# DIRECT MARKETING

CRAIN
BOOKS

**Crain Books**
740 North Rush Street
Chicago, Illinois 60611

ISBN: 0-87251-052-2

Library of Congress Catalog Card Number: 80-67813

1   2   3   4   5   6

Published by Crain Books, division of Crain Communications, Inc. All rights
reserved. This book may not be reproduced in whole or in part in any form or
by any means without written permission from the publisher.

Printed in the United States of America

# Contents

```
```

# Introduction

To aficionados, it's known simply as Section 2, although some wags initially tagged it Section 8. It first appeared January 1, 1979, as a new center pullout section in *Advertising Age*.

The initial concept still holds. It was developed to provide in-depth coverage of a specific marketing topic—a different topic each week, one not normally covered by *Ad Age,* or covered only minimally. The Section was designed to be pulled out and retained as a ready reference.

And indeed it was.

Reader response was phenomenal. Requests poured in for reprints of specific articles, of entire Sections, to the point where *Advertising Age* was unable to fulfill the requests. Obviously you, the advertising/marketing person, have a hunger for certain information not easily obtainable from other sources. This book, one of a series, is our attempt to meet that need.

This book is not merely a reprint of a specific Section 2. Rather it is a compilation, a gleaning, of all the Section 2 information applicable to the topic at hand. Every effort has been made to ensure that the information included is relevant and up-to-date.

I hope that it will aid you in your work—and more, that you will enjoy reading it.

**Kathryn Sederberg**
**Director, Crain Books**

# A Journey Through Time

## BY BOB STONE

CHICAGO—It's been only a scant 12 years since Pete Hoke Jr., publisher of the leading trade journal in his field, changed its name from *Reporter of Direct Mail* to *Direct Marketing Magazine*. It wasn't until 1973—only seven years ago—that the Direct Mail Advertising Assn. changed its name to Direct Mail/Marketing Assn. Yet the roots of direct marketing started to form just 22 years after the signing of the Declaration of Independence.

### The First Trial Offer

History reveals the "father" of the free trial offer, bastion of direct marketing offers, was a Connecticut custom clock maker by the name of Eli Terry. (His neighbor, by the way, was Eli Whitney.) In 1798 Mr. Terry set off across the wintry hills of the Connecticut River Valley on a sales trip seeking buyers for his clocks among the farmers.

Mr. Terry struck a unique bargain with the doubting farmers he approached. He would leave his clock on trial. If it gave good service he would collect payment on his next trip along the route; if the clock proved faulty, the customer would "owe him nothing." Thus Eli Terry became the first manufacturer and seller, so far as is known, to offer merchandise on a free-trial, no-risk, no-money-down, approval basis.

---

*Bob Stone is chairman, Stone & Adler, Chicago.*

But Eli Terry's innovations didn't stop with the free trial offer. He had yet another surprise for those prospects who liked his clocks, but lacked the $25 he had set as his price. He reasoned he could double or triple his sales if he accepted a small down payment and arranged to collect regular installments on each of his trips. So far as can be determined, Eli Terry was the first man to push installment buying. Terry's wisdom has withstood 182 years of marketing history. Selling under the installment method is a keystone to success for many major direct marketers to this day.

### The Mail Order House

In 1872, the "father" of the catalog discovered the appeal of direct mail. His name: Aaron Montgomery Ward. But his first effort was not a catalog. It was a single sheet, unillustrated price list offering farmers savings of 40%. Farmers responded in great numbers.

By 1884, just 12 years after that first single sheet had appeared, Ward was producing a 240-page catalog containing 10,000 items. He guaranteed satisfaction, or your money back, thus establishing a basic tenet for the thousands of catalogs to follow.

Two years later, 1886, marked the historic launch of what was to become Sears, Roebuck & Co. Young Richard Warren Sears was a telegraph operator in a railroad and express office of the Minneapolis and St. Louis line at North Redwood, Minn., a village of three houses.

Finding himself in possession of a shipment of undeliverable watches, Sears accepted an offer to buy these $25 gold-filled watches for only $12 each. Sears reasoned the best prospects would be other railroad agents, men who swore by the correct time. He had the perfect list to support his reasoning—a targeted list of 20,000 station agents. It was from this "accidental" beginning that the world's greatest catalog operation grew.

Joseph Spiegel entered the catalog business in 1905, being the first to sell by mail on "easy credit terms." It was the same kind of offer Eli Terry had made in person and for the same reasons. Spiegel catalog copy read, "We are willing to trust you indefinitely . . . and to receive our pay by the month, so that no purchase is a burden." (Sears followed with credit terms in 1911.)

Ward, Sears and Spiegel all offered a wide assortment of merchandise—thousands of items not

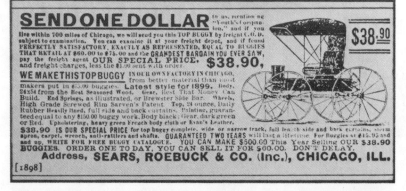

**Early examples of direct marketing sales tools include Montgomery Ward catalog that depicts the retailer as a "busy bee hive" of merchandise, a Burpee seed catalog and an ad for a Sears Roebuck buggy.**

generally available in the small towns springing up all over America. But in the interim a new catalog phenomenon emerged— specialized catalogs designed to cater to specialized needs and interests.

Henry Field Seed Nursery, for example, was established in 1892. The legendary L. L. Bean was founded in 1912. Today there are hundreds and hundreds of special interest catalogs.

Neiman-Marcus of Dallas will always have a prominent place in the history of catalogs. It distributed its very first Christmas catalog outside its trading area in the early 1950s, foreshadowing a trend toward selling upscale merchandise via the catalog method nationwide. The trend became an avalanche following Roger Horchow's introduction of the Horchow Collection in 1974.

## Books

As we continue to chart history it becomes evident the thirst for knowledge through books led naturally to distribution through direct marketing methods.

In American cities bookstores were among the first shops to open for business. But in villages and rural areas bookstores were almost unknown. The sales of books were dependent upon the peddler and on mail order advertising. Books sold well. The "New England Primer," for example, sold over 1,000,000 copies. Webster's "Blue Book Speller" sold 65,000,000 copies in 34 years.

A major milestone in the direct marketing saga occurred in 1926 when Harry Sherman and Maxwell Sackheim founded the Book-of-the-Month Club, based upon a unique marketing concept involving the negative option method of selling books.

Time-Life books was launched in 1961. And its marketing concept— continuity series—was the foundation for building one of the world's largest book publishing companies. It is estimated that Time-Life

Books worldwide sales for the year 1979 exceeded a quarter of a billion dollars.

## Pioneer Developers

No history of direct marketing would be complete without mentioning a few of the pioneers who had the vision to see the opportunities inherent in direct marketing methods.

John H. Patterson founded National Cash Register Co. in the 1800s. He was the first to use direct mail to get qualified leads for sales people. Today, with the cost of an industrial call exceeding $90, the need for qualified leads is even greater.

Homer J. Buckley—he coined the term "direct mail"—founded Buckley-Dement & Co. in Chicago in 1905. His company was the first to offer professional direct mail creative services.

In 1921 Leonard J. Raymond founded Dickie-Raymond. Leonard established the principle that it made good sense for major corporations to use a direct mail advertising agency in addition to a general advertising agency.

Prominent in the 1950s were Maxwell Sackheim and Vic Schwab, two pioneers in direct response print advertising. Those who had gotten leads and orders by direct mail alone were beginning to discover the efficiency of print.

## The Fabulous '50s

Now the pace quickens. The "Fabulous '50s," more than any other decade, saw direct marketing take quantum leaps forward.

Diners Club, the first t&e card, started in 1950. What was to become Master Charge likewise started in 1950. (The American Express credit card wasn't introduced until 1965.) It was the availability of credit through the medium of charge cards that enabled direct marketers to sell big ticket items in volume for the first time without fear of massive credit losses. Today American Express numbers 10,000,000 card holders; Diners

Club  4,000,000;  Visa  over
44,000,000; Master Charge over
47,000,000.

Concurrent with the credit card
explosion was the proliferation of
computers. Putting lists on computers opened up unparalleled opportunities for segmented marketing.

A major breakthrough occurred
for direct response magazine advertising in 1959. The breakthrough was a four-page bind-in
centerfold insert in *TV Guide* with
a perforated business reply card
for Columbia Record Club. Wunderman, Ricotta & Kline, today the
world's largest direct marketing
agency, created this breakthrough
concept. Response was sensational
in comparison to run-of-magazine
advertising.

## Innovations of the '60s

The momentum of the '50s car-
ried right into the '60s. And "Ma
Bell"—AT&T Long Lines—was a
major contributor. AT&T introduced Inward WATS (now called
800 Service) in 1961. For the first
time the consumer could call toll-
free from anywhere in the country
to order merchandise, or get information. Direct marketers found

their average phone order to be
about 20% larger than the average
mail order.

Another unlikely contributor to
the direct marketing explosion was
the U.S. Postal Service, which
made sorting mail by Zip code
mandatory on Jan. 1, 1967. Most
members of the direct marketing
fraternity viewed Zip code sorting
as an unwarranted expense and
marketing, Old American Insurance Co., Kansas City, Mo., took
the view that Zip codes as market
segments constitute ideal homogeneous consumer groupings. He
was right! Today the Baier Zip
code marketing concept is standard operating procedure among
direct marketers.

The '60s also saw direct marketers "discovering" tv. Back in
1961 Aaron Adler, who later was to
become a cofounder of Stone &
Adler, was involved in developing
the famed Vegamatic tv commercial.

Early direct marketing commercials were "low budget," using
pitchmen for the most part. But as
major companies entered the direct marketing stream, commercials improved. *Reader's Digest*
produced its first commercial in

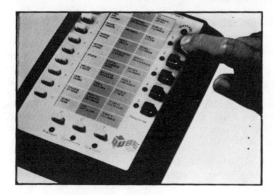

**This mail order book ad appeared in 1882 and promoted "The Science of Life." The Qube keyboard allows viewers to respond immediately to what they see on tv.**

burden. But in the January-February, 1967, issue of *Harvard Business Review,* an article titled "Zip Code ... New Tool For Marketers" took quite a different view.

The author, Martin Baier, vp-support of a mass mailing in 1969, finding that tv support hypoed response from its prime medium. Today tv support is used widely for newspaper inserts. And direct sell tv is used by major publishers and a variety of companies selling merchandise to the consumer.

## The '70s and Beyond

The '70s was a time of "coming together" for direct marketing. With all the tools in place, major marketers found the "accountable advertising" aspect appealing. And many set up direct marketing departments as separate profit centers. Major general advertising agencies acquired direct marketing agencies to better serve their clients' total needs.

As the 1970 decade came to a close, the Direct Mail/Marketing Assn. estimated total sales of goods and services for 1979 reached $87 billion. Not bad!

Now, as we enter the '80s, direct marketers eagerly look forward to new tools: Interactive tv, cable tv, Viewtron, videodiscs and developments yet to come.

Thank you, Eli Terry!

# The Ever-Present Medium

BY CAROL GALGINAITIS

CHICAGO—Check out your mailbox. Turn on your tv. Open your newspaper.

If you have functioning eyes and ears, and maintain at least minimal contact with society, it's hard to remain oblivious to the number and variety of products currently being sold through direct marketing, a term loosely defined to refer to any technique which eliminates the middleman.

Upon hearing this phrase, the unsophisticated may envision the "Have I got a gadget for you!" genre of late night tv commercials or the small ads in the back pages of magazines offering products generally delivered in plain brown wrappers.

But the industry is far more diverse; "statement stuffers" accompanying monthly bills, Sunday supplements crammed with cents-off coupons, letters seeking donations for universities and charities, glossy catalogs depicting exotic, expensive gifts, and telephone solicitors selling newspaper subscriptions are all common examples.

These approaches, although admittedly varied, share many characteristics. They all combine the advertising and merchandising aspects of marketing; they are based upon the concept of segmentation, and they offer opportunities for closely monitoring sales, and therefore effectiveness. And they also share something else: Evidence of phenomenal growth. Although direct marketing is hardly a new concept (Montgomery Ward offered catalog sales with money-back guarantees as early as 1875), the last decade has seen dramatic increases in sales. According to the Direct Mail/Marketing Assn. (DMMA), 1978 sales figures reached $87 billion, a 45% increase in three years; Robert Stone, chairman of Chicago-based Stone & Adler, predicts that this figure will approach $120 billion by 1981.

DMMA also reports that in 1977, 70% of all magazine subscriptions and 25% of all book sales were made through direct marketing. Even more remarkable, telephone sales leapfrogged from $22,000,000 in 1969 to $500,000,000 in 1978, making it the fastest growing area in the industry.

The statistics continue to titillate the profit-hungry mind. Maxwell Sroge, a mail order business development, advertising and consulting company located in Chicago, reports that the 7% after tax profit ratio of publicly held mail order companies (for 1978) compares very favorably with the 2.5% reported for retailers and the 5.4% reported for manufacturers. Furthermore, retailers who add direct marketing operations often find that their in-store sales actually increase.

"When Bell & Howell first started offering cameras by direct mail, retailers initially objected," reports Jerold L. Heisler, manager of the consumer marketing services division of the Market Development Corp. "Then, they saw that everyone's business improved.

"Let's say that 2% to 5% of those

mailed information bought cameras," Mr. Heisler said. "Then, those [others] who got the material would go to dealers to buy that or another model. So the mailing served the purpose of advertising to those who chose not to order by mail, and the effort supplemented rather than replaced retail sales."

"What we are seeing here at Bloomingdale's is that we are tap-

ping a whole new audience, people who are literally outside our area," recounts Doreen McCurley, direct response marketing director for the New York-based retailer. "People in Texas, California, where we have no retail stores, are buying from our catalog. Our image is reaching out nationally, with no decrease in our floor traffic."

Obviously such occurrences create great excitement in the market-

Airline flight magazines are popular places for direct marketers to advertise. The ads often specialize in travel-oriented items and usually carry coupons or toll-free phone numbers.

ing world as analysts attempt to predict the future by understanding the past. Since effective merchants must continually respond to changing life styles, many study sociological trends for explanations.

"One cause for this tremendous growth is the increase in the number of working women," says Robert DeLay, president of DMMA. "Right now, almost 50% of the eligible women are working outside the home. People simply are tired of spending their leisure time buying necessities. If they could get groceries by mail, I'm sure they would."

"Anyone with limited time is a prime target," agrees Market Development Corp.'s Mr. Heisler. "Doctors have always been good direct market buyers. They have no time and lots of money.

"Furthermore," he continues, "we are seeing the decline of the small independent merchant. As more and more stores become self-service or discount centers, customers find that service is increasingly poor. Then, when they have the hassle of traffic and parking—who wouldn't find direct marketing more convenient? You can study a catalog in the quiet of your own home, and select merchandise at your leisure."

And save gasoline in the process.

"The limited gas supply has to lead to rising direct marketing sales," says Donna Sweeney, publicity coordinator for DMMA. "Another result is that the suburban shopping malls, which rely heavily on passenger car traffic, will suffer. So a lot of retailers are getting into catalog sales. They need to respond to changes in the market."

Another trend involves consumers' growing trust in the direct marketing process. "Years ago there was resistance to buying expensive goods without seeing them, and customers wouldn't send a check to someone they never had heard of," says Mr. Heisler. "Now, more and more rep-

utable companies are involved, which builds confidence among consumers."

In fact, customers are not only willing to buy without firsthand examination, they are also often paying for the privilege.

Direct marketing's appeal is "more a matter of convenience and selection than cost savings," says Ray Haase, vp of Old Equity Life and past president of the Chicago Assn. of Direct Marketing. "People buying through direct marketing don't get any real cost breaks."

But obviously, industry honesty and excellence are important elements in consumer participation.

"Quality and service are vital to our success," explains Jack Miller, president of the Quill Corp., a discount office supply house located in Northbrook, Ill. "In addition to our 'Customers Bill of Rights' which we include in our catalog, we also enclose a form in every shipment with detailed instructions for returning the product if the customer isn't satisfied.

"Sure, you have to make it easy for people to shop, but you also have to make it easy for them to return merchandise if it's not what they wanted or expected. After all, if we don't get repeat business, we can forget the whole deal."

In addition, many technological changes have had great impact on the industry. The advent of 800 phone numbers and widespread access to credit have made it much more convenient for customers to order.

Major bank cards such as Visa, American Express and Master Charge also offer the merchant some reassurance about his customer's credit-worthiness, and have contributed to direct marketers' offering more and more expensive items.

■ But the industry, like any marketing outfit, faces the problem of identifying those consumers most likely to respond to the direct marketing approach. The relatively recent introduction of computerized, segmented lists, however, has greatly facilitated the process.

"Computers allow very sophisticated analysis," says Mr. Heisler. "Many companies now compile lists of consumers based upon their previous buying history, their buying frequency, the type of product they ordered and the amount they spent. This works because we've seen that people who bought through direct marketing once are more likely to buy again."

"Now we can really pinpoint our audience," agrees Ms. Sweeney of DMMA. "And there are virtually thousands of marketplaces out there!"

These marketplaces are also becoming easier and easier to reach. WATS lines have substantially cut the costs of telephoning homes and businesses nationwide, while Zip codes provide another way to analyze geographic location by approximate socioeconomic status.

■ It doesn't take sharp businesspersons long to realize that these factors all point toward continued growth, so many ad agencies are forming direct response divisions. Some, like Compton Direct Marketing (CDM) of New York have experienced such dramatic increases in billings that it almost defies credibility.

Says Jerome Lieb, president of the 10-year-old CDM, "When I joined in 1977, we did more business in one year than all the previous years combined. We increased the billings six times over in 1978, and doubled them again in 1979."

"There just aren't enough agencies to handle the business," says Mr. DeLay with a marked note of ambivalence. "All the agencies have too much business to handle. It's my impression," says Mr. DeLay, "that several of them turn down three accounts for every one they take. And places like Stone & Adler have increased their number of employes by 60%. Now that's real growth."

But such rapid development does not come without headaches, and many believe that the No. 1 problem confronting the industry is the lack of adequately trained personnel.

"The precept of direct marketing is that everything is trackable," says Mr. Stone. "We keep a balance sheet on everything, and discipline is very strong.

"In general advertising, the prime object is image or remembrance. In direct marketing, we must improve our product image, but we are always worried about the bottom line. If you are trained in general advertising, your philosophy is just different."

To meet these personnel needs, many of the direct marketing companies and professional associations offer training seminars. DMMA alone is doing $1,000,000 in training programs per year, and, says Mr. DeLay, is "literally besieged by requests from places like IBM, McGraw-Hill and ITT." In addition, influential industry leaders—like Robert Stone—are encouraging colleges to develop direct marketing programs.

"Fifteen universities now offer courses, to varying degrees," he says. "Our goal is to have 100 more colleges add programs within the next five years."

And a few direct marketing placements, such as Gillick, Ridenour & Associates of Chicago have sprung up in the last several years.

Despite their creative approaches to many industry problems, however, direct marketers have not yet found the solution to inflation. Paper costs are escalating, and, although mail fees are currently stable, they have increased substantially over the years. But curiously, direct marketing is less vulnerable than are other marketing techniques to periodic downturns in the economy.

"In times of economic hardship," says Mr. Lieb, "people don't go out to the stores, and many direct marketing products are oriented toward home use. For instance, the Book-of-the-Month Club started in

1926 and continued to grow during the Great Depression. Furthermore, direct marketing is geared toward the impulse purchase. When you're sitting at home and get this catalog, it somehow is easier to 'justify' the expense."

No such silver lining appears in the government regulation cloud, and most feel that outside intervention is both annoying and unnecessary.

"The DMMA does a hell of a good job in making people [in the industry] conscientious," explains Ms. McCurley. "Everyone realizes that honesty and service are vital to our existence."

■ Many companies voluntarily offer their customers the choice to remain off any mailing lists. "Furthermore, the DMMA's Mail Preference Service, which is well promoted through magazines and tv, provides a mechanism by which customers can get their names off lists," says Mr. Heisler.

"Interestingly, the number of complaints is infinitesimal, and more people ask to be put on the lists than ask to be removed. Most of the privacy legislation aimed at making lists unavailable is based on misguided consumerism."

Future developments?

■ "Direct marketing was never a good thing with a generalized audience," says Mr. Haase, "and mail order used to be the only way to target your market. Now direct marketing can and will grow within any medium which allows you to segment.

"For instance, specialized magazines appealing to very specific audiences are prime. But cable tv will be the largest growth area. It not only offers more air time, but it also is structured around specialized

channeling. "Just look at QUBE [a two-way cable system currently being test marketed in Columbus, O.], added Mr. Haase. "It allows people sitting at home to vote, to order merchandise advertised on tv. It offers a way to get measurable, immediate response."

■ In addition to cable, Ms. Sweeney forecasts continued increases in telephone sales. "People still want that personal contact," she says. "They like to be able to ask, 'What does it really look like?'"

"We will see growth in the number of companies getting involved in direct marketing," predicts Mr. Lieb, "especially among the Fortune 500 companies. Major retailers will get into it not just to encourage traffic into their stores, but also to develop new profit centers."

Mr. Stone foresees that service-oriented business, particularly financial institutions, are ripe for development. "There is such a scramble for money, and general advertising just is not doing it." And because of the increased convenience of phone and mail order, Mr. DeLay looks for big opportunities in the industrial area.

■ But whether the most impressive growth occurs in cable or telephone, consumer or industrial, it is obvious that the experts are convinced that they're backing a winner.

"Growth in the '70s will be nothing compared to what will happen in the '80s," concludes Ms. Sweeney.

■ "In fact," adds Mr. Lieb, "I am convinced that the majority of shopping 10 years from today will be done through direct marketing."

# Ethics Enter the Picture

**BY THEODORE J. GAGE**

CHICAGO—"If I live in an apartment, and I get flyers from a roofing company—that's junk mail. But I like outdoor things, and when I get an L.L. Bean catalog in the mail—that sure isn't junk mail to me."

John M. Cavanaugh, director of ethical practices for the Direct Mail/Marketing Assn. (DMMA) uses this example to define irrelevant, or junk, mail. But consumers getting mail in which they have no interest is only one part of the question of ethics in direct marketing.

Newspaper consumer columns are full of letters from people who haven't gotten what they expected from a direct marketing company.

Yet quality companies like Sears, Roebuck & Co., Marshall Field & Co. and L.L. Bean have thousands of satisfied customers and have helped build direct marketing into a $75 billion industry.

But the gray area between poor service—even fraud—and completely honest and quality service is broad. That's where ethics enters the picture. A number of direct marketing associations exist, and one of the most influential is the DMMA. It has a code of ethics to which many member companies, list brokers, managers, list managers and marketing companies adhere.

Because direct marketing companies have strongly resisted any form or suggestion of government regulation, the industry has established a number of guidelines to curb potential abuses. But in the mid-1970s, the federal government decided to hold hearings to determine whether "junk" mail and other direct marketing approaches infringed on citizens' privacy.

When the Privacy Protection Study Commission finished its "Report On Mailing Lists" in mid-1977, it was far from an indictment of the industry. Ronald Plesser, a Washington, D.C., attorney and legal advisor to the privacy commission, says, "We didn't find anything out-of-control.

"We recommended a voluntary approach to allow people to get off and stay off mailing lists. Of course, we didn't deal with outright fraud in direct marketing—the Postal Service and the Federal Trade Commission already control that aspect."

Members of the DMMA and similar marketing associations regulate themselves with guidelines. The DMMA, for example, requires members to make offers clear and honest, never to slander, never to mislead the consumer or try to trick him, never to make a free offer that wasn't actually free, to make telephone solicitations at reasonable hours and so on.

"We have given our members rules and a way to regulate themselves—and they do," says Mr. Cavanaugh. "They also have ways to get off mailing lists. Magazines provide boxes and credit card companies provide ways for people to keep from getting direct marketing information.

"It's important to mention, though, that few people contact us to get their names off lists. In fact, most people who write us ask to receive information about things they're interested in."

Robert Stone, chairman of Stone & Adler, says "the caliber of the direct marketing industry—including ethics—is rapidly improving. As more top, upscale companies get deeper into the business, the level of the business rises. There is hardly any room today for slam-bang operators."

# A Not-So-Silent Salesman

**BY THEODORE J. GAGE**

CHICAGO—It is, perhaps, this century's last frontier of mass advertising. It is the silent salesman that patiently waits on your office desk or in your living room, poised to deliver a pitch.

For our society, it has become a convenience, if not a necessity. It is loved and hated. It is a friend, but also an intruder. The telephone is all of these things.

Because it allows personal contact and is cost-efficient, the phone will almost certainly become an increasingly popular marketing tool in the 1980s. And its use may spark more debate—and more excitement—than has any other method of direct marketing.

Telephone marketing is young compared to direct mail, and only in the past few years has it received significant attention as a major medium. Postal rates have soared, printing and paper costs have made direct mail marketing more expensive than ever. And sending sales people randomly to business and residential customers has become far too costly for most companies.

The fastest growing segment of the business is response, or incoming calls. Many print and broadcast sales appeals offer customers the option of responding by mail or phone. "As a clerical, response function, [use of] the telephone has exploded," says Edward Blank, president of Edward Blank Associates, New York.

"Collect calling and toll-free 800 numbers are increasing rapidly. It's easier and quicker for the customer." Credit cards have made it relatively safe for both parties to transact business by telephone, and telephone marketing experts say consumers often enjoy and feel more secure talking to someone about a product before they buy.

But the segment dealing with outgoing calls—telephone solicitations aimed at businesses and consumers—offers the greatest potential for market growth. It has caught the attention of consumer groups and the federal government as concerns about right to privacy have arisen.

"For the 1980s, the telephone is the medium," says Murray Roman, who has been in telephone marketing for more than 20 years. Some people in the industry consider him the father of direct telephone marketing. "This is an exciting era for the telephone."

The telephone marketers' enthusiasm, however, may be tempered by objections stemming from consumers' right to privacy.

On Dec. 6, 1979, the first bill dealing directly with telephone solicitation was introduced in the U.S. Congress. Rep. Lester Aspin (D., Wis.), along with 81 cosponsors, submitted a bill entitled the "Telephone Privacy Act" (HR 6047) that would regulate the direct telephone marketing business.

It has four basic points:

**1.** All public telephone companies must give their customers at least one chance a year to express a preference not to receive "unsolicited commercial telephone calls." They would probably do so by checking a box on their monthly telephone bills.

**2.** Any marketing company making such calls to businesses or consumers would be required to obtain a list of these "negative preference" customers from the telephone companies.

**3.** Fines up to $1,000 per violation would be imposed on companies found not complying with the above regulations. As a safeguard to the marketing companies, only U.S. attorneys could file charges and the government would need at least 10 complaints against a company before it could press charges.

**4.** The cost to the telephone companies for maintaining the "negative preference" list would be distributed among the marketing companies.

In certain ways, the bill resembles something direct mail marketers have done for the past few years—given people the option of checking boxes on subscription notices or notifying the Direct Mail/Marketing Assn. that they don't wish to receive solicitations through the mail.

Telephone marketers speak of instituting similar self-regulatory procedures. But if Rep. Aspin's bill or something similar passes, the Federal Communications Commission would ensure compliance. The earliest congressional hearings on the Telephone Privacy Act would be early June, 1980.

In related action, the FCC has been looking into the direct telephone marketing business since March, 1978, conducting research and gathering public opinion and testimony. "The commission feels [the issue] merits investigation," says an FCC spokesman. "We have made no decisions or recommendations—we're just addressing the question." An FCC response to this investigation may appear as early as February.

Any "solution" to the questions surrounding telephone marketing will probably cause a stir. On one

hand, there is a strong argument that direct marketers have a constitutional right to use the phone.

"Any marketer worthy of the name would look at the mail and the telephone as a right," says Mr. Roman. On the other hand, there's a valid argument that citizens have the right to privacy—to have telephones in their homes and offices without getting calls from sales people if they don't wish to receive them.

"It's the kind of issue everyone wishes would go away," says one federal communications expert. "We're dealing with tough constitutional questions on both sides. No matter what solution you come up with, somebody's going to feel his constitutional rights have been infringed upon."

■ Marketers must grapple with a number of questions as the phone becomes a more attractive marketing tool. One is: When should a company solicit customers by telephone and who should be solicited?

"Personally, I would hesitate to phone people who haven't shown some [previous] interest in my client or his product," says Robert Stone, chairman of Stone & Adler, a full-service direct marketing company. "If a customer has dealt with the firm before, then I think he would usually have an interest in hearing from the company.

"But phoning someone who has never dealt with you before, just because they've shown a preference for a certain type of product or have a certain life style, I don't know ..."

The divergent opinions in the marketing industry are obvious. Young & Rubicam, which owns Stone & Adler, recently plunged head first into the telephone marketing business by starting Direct Marketing Services Inc., a division of Wunderman, Ricotta & Kline, which it also owns.

Mr. Stone's view is shared by a number of direct marketing experts who use the mail freely but hesitate to use the telephone in the same way. "As far as mail's concerned, the garbage can is only an arm's length away," says one marketing exec.

■ "Mail is pretty inoffensive. But the phone—especially if certain companies use persistent operators—can be a real and unavoidable nuisance."

The U.S. Postal Service estimates that the average American gets about three pieces of direct mail a week, and the Direct Mail/Marketing Assn. says in its "Fact Book" that "this amount can hardly be called a 'glut' as some writers have termed it."

But if telephone marketing grows as predicted and the average American gets three or more calls a week from solicitors—will that constitute a service or an invasion of privacy?

"Most people don't object to receiving calls about something worthwhile," says Mr. Blank. Although his company makes more than 2,000,000 calls a year, he says few people are hostile to the operators.

The majority of consumers aren't interested in a particular product or service, as expected. But when a consumer says he or she isn't interested, Mr. Blank says "we instruct our operators not to be persistent—they just say 'thank you very much' and 'goodbye.'"

■ Advocates of telephone marketing argue that if people objected to it as much as the federal government fears, the business wouldn't have grown so rapidly. "If people don't respond to telephone, or any kind of marketing, it isn't going to last very long," says Les Wunderman, chairman of Wunderman, Ricotta & Kline.

"When we call people, we have done good enough research to target our audiences and hit people who have an interest in our call. Irrelevant phoning is just too bloody expensive to keep up for very long."

Although the sophisticated, reputable marketing companies will probably not offend consumers, the telephone marketing experts admit that the telephone can be abused by hard-sell outfits. "In the end, a few of those companies could severely damage our industry [telephone marketing], our reputation and our effectiveness," says one exec.

# TV Response—It Works For the Experts

**BY ANNA SOBCZYNSKI**

CHICAGO—It chops, it peels, it dices and it serves at table.

It even lights your cigaret while it soothes you with Elvis' Golden Moldies.

It is the ultimate gadget tv direct marketers dream of. Guaranteed to dazzle and beguile the viewer, to make him want to pick up the phone and order one for each member of his extremely large family, it sweeps the country in a matter of days.

But then it sweeps itself right OUT of the marketplace just as quickly.

Such seems to be the fate of direct marketers on television. Relying on precarious success at best, they capitalize on the human desire to desire—to "must have" on impulse. Thus, they must also be ready for people to change their minds against buying the item just as abruptly as they wished to have it.

The picture is not all gloomy, but tv direct marketing seems to have seen its heyday. To be sure, there are still many flourishing companies around doing a brisk business. But there are others, even the giants of the field, who are barely limping along or who have had to escape from the airwaves in order to survive.

Why do some companies make it while others, offering almost identical merchandise, fold? What is the over-all diagnosis of the tv direct sale business and what is its prognosis?

The answer to the first question is simple. In order to make tv direct sales successful, it is important to diversify and it is important to specialize. If that answer seems contradictory, that's because it accurately reflects the complexity of the business.

Some attribute their winning streak to having kept their options open. By offering a myriad of different types of products, if one should fail, there's always another to fall back on. Other masters of fortune insist that specialization is the answer because then the company is identified as the leader and expert in what it offers.

■ Ronco, one of the heavies in the business, sells records as well as about 15 other products on the air, including items from the hardware, houseware, electrical and electronic fields. Such diversity has doubled Ronco's profits in the last three years. Net sales last year totaled $30,000,000, while after-tax income was $500,000.

Ronco's $8,000,000 advertising budget is spent exclusively on tv. According to Jerry Epstein, Ronco's vice-president: "Our products are unique and affordable. When things [the economy] get bad, our business goes up." It must be doing something right. It has been turning a profit for 15 years.

At the other end of the sale spectrum is Lakeshore Music. In business a brief 3½ years, Lakeshore doubled in size last year, boasting net sales of $15,000,000 with $4,000,000 being spent to purchase television time. Ninety-eight per cent of its budget goes into tv.

Unlike Ronco with its multiple item offers, Lakeshore not only specializes in records, it specializes, would you believe, in records that offer music for truck drivers. A current top-seller is an album called "Road Music," which is a compilation of truck driver hits.

Although the records are mostly country and western, the names Dolly Parton, Johnny Cash and Tammy Wynette aren't part of Lakeshore's hit parade. Does the name Nell Street ring a bell? It does if you know REAL country and western. "Down-home funky country" is what Don Mundo, owner of Lakeshore Music, calls it. It's certainly brought him down-home, funky profits.

■ Television direct sale is not a new phenomenon. Popeil Bros. has been around for nearly 30 years, making its name in unique gadgetry. It has made words like Pocket Fisherman and Veg-o-Matic household terms.

Yet even this granddaddy of direct marketing floundered somewhere along the line and nearly fell. The declining business' stock was recently puchased by T.S.P. Corp., a Florida-based company headed by Saul Padek. Since the purchase, Popeil reports an upswing.

■ However, television sales are not a part of its current campaign to get back on its feet, nor do they figure in for the immediate future. "Instead, the company is consolidating and moving out excess inventory and developing its product lines," says Charles R. Cump, vp-marketing and sales. Popeil is now involved in manufacturing and distribution. Although television is not being ruled out for the future,

the company wants to keep its options open for the time being.

Brookville Marketing, a formidable contender in television direct marketing, has been assigned a Chapter 11 category of the bankruptcy code. Under this provision, the struggling company is given a second chance to make a go of it. Should it fail, bankruptcy will be declared and the company's assets liquidated.

Brookville ran a successful business selling records, magazines, books and exercise equipment as part of its diverse product line on television. It won't be selling records anymore, revealed Barry Rosen, media director for Greybark Advertising, Brookville's in-house ad agency.

Mr. Rosen explained: "Altogether, tv sales are not as profitable as they once were." The company which sold nearly 5,000,000 Elvis Presley post-mortem hit record collections, is now selling *Prevention* subscriptions on the air, as well as several other publications, including *Soap Opera Digest*.

■ Whether a company chooses to specialize or diversify is not the sole determinant that makes 'em or breaks 'em. That would be too easy and who said *that* was easy? Tv direct marketing companies exhibit a symptom which has also been the downfall of many other businesses: Oversaturation of the market. Once a company has sold 5,000,000 Elvis records and its competitor has sold 5,000,000 more, where can it go from there?

"Once you saturate the country with a hit," says Brookville's Mr. Rosen, "it burns itself out. There are not all that many records left to be done." Companies like Brookville have sold compilations of single artist greatest hits and music centered around a theme such as black gospel music. But once they've taken all "the greatest hits of," "memorable moments in" and "never-to-be-forgotten milestones," there comes a time when there just aren't anymore. What started out as six or seven companies selling this type of music-via-television successfully turned into 40 or 50 companies having to sell out a short time later.

The same goes for gadgets.

"Intensive advertising of nonrecord products was a relatively new phenomenon here in the country in the late '60s, early '70s," explains David Catlin, vp and general manager of K-Tel whose Imperial House division currently sells music products via the tube.

"Now that novelty has worn off. Many other companies entered the direct marketing business because they didn't have an organization capable of distributing to stores," Mr. Catlin adds.

Not only did these companies proliferate like mushrooms after a rain, they also ran headfirst into a general economic slowdown throughout the country. Those in the record sales part of the business got hit especially hard because of the particular slowdown in the record business. Add to that a drastic rise in the cost of television time (a hefty 30% to 40% in the past year in some cases, according to one source) and the formula spells trouble for the television direct marketing business.

Most companies purchase the least expensive television time. They run their commercials during the day or late at night and stay away from prime time and fringe. The direct response companies also look for spot buys. Spot advertising may be cheaper, but it's also unreliable. Spots get bumped off the air if someone else is willing to buy the time at a higher rate. The companies get a rain check, of course, but have no control over when their commercial will air.

Direct marketing ads proliferate during January and February. They come on when everyone else has gone home following television's Christmas Party blitz. The rates are cheaper and the airwaves less crowded. This year,

however, the companies will find themselves locked elbow-to-elbow for air space, even in the off-season months. Between the upcoming Olympic high hurdles and political campaign below-the-belts, direct marketers will be brutally squeezed out of many advertising schedules.

This will affect not only first-quarter tv time buys, but will become even more acute for the July-August period, also traditionally direct-marketing time.

And because the business is predicated on television commercials, this could be its most trying and telling year yet. The only solution is to buy time as early as possible and be willing to pay higher rates.

"We can't cut back on television time, because a good schedule is a good schedule. You can't reduce it by 20% and expect to get the same effectiveness in the marketplace," explains Mr. Catlin of K-Tel.

Time is easier to get and often cheaper on independent stations than network affiliates. Those companies that operate in Canada face an additional problem. "The Canadian business is a nice little business but there are few tv stations available," explains Victor Lindeman, President of V & R Advertising, one of the oldest direct response companies. It has been in business for 28 years.

The inflation situation has affected the business in several other ways as well. Credit cards have become the American way of life. In order to survive in the marketplace, direct response companies must accept credit cards—usually Visa and Master Charge.

The plastic payment cards, however, carry a hefty price tag. Credit card companies want 4% of the retail selling price, according to one source. Besides that, most direct response offers are for relatively low-price items. Thus, because of the manpower, facilities and outlay necessary, credit card sales don't pay in the direct response business.

Because cash is scarce, a third method has evolved which has both simplified and hurt the business. C.O.D. (collect-on-delivery) makes it possible for the interested viewer to order an item which attracted his attention on television and wait to pay the postman when it arrives. Unfortunately for the business, the postman often comes back empty-handed. That is, he returns with what he was supposed to have left behind. It's come to be known as the C.O.D. Rejection Factor and it has hurt the business substantially.

"C.O.D. refusals have been creeping up very strongly in the last five years," claims Wesley Wood, co-owner of Candlelite Music, the largest independent marketer of records and tapes in the U.S. and Canada. "Eight years ago the tv business was all prepaid. Now 50% of it is C.O.D. People just don't have the money," Mr. Woods adds.

"A distributor loses $3 to $4 dollars minimum on a C.O.D. rejection," claims David Catlin of K-Tel. "It's often the difference between a profit or a loss on a particular promotion."

People do still have the desire to buy via direct response, mainly because it's convenient. Television, however, may not be the airwave of the future. It's just as convenient to order from a catalog. And because it's all prepaid, there is no 'C.O.D. Rejection Factor' to complicate profits. So in the face of rising television costs, the high competitiveness of the business and a dwindling supply of 'oldies' records and ingenious gadgets, formerly exclusive tv-reliant companies are turning toward the direct mail business—in droves.

■ K-Tel's Imperial House plans to go the direct mail route, recognizing it as the direct response direction of the future. Candlelite Music, which continues to do tv commercials, is already doing 20,000,000 mailings per year via direct mail offers as well. And the mail order part of Candlelite's business is growing while the tube is on the decline.

Some items sell better via direct mail than they do on tv. Besides records, Candlelite sells limited edition porcelain plates and figurines via mail order. It tried selling a Norman Rockwell plate on television, but it didn't work.

Wesley Wood cites two reasons why: "Items such as records," he says, "are more broad-based in appeal than collectibles." Also, he adds, "There is only so much you can charge for an item on tv." While a record costs $6.98, plates start at $9.98 and can go as high as $24.98 and up. Mr. Wood predicts that collectibles are one of the largest-growing segments of the mail order business. Not only can a distributor sell more high-price items via mail, but he can sell multiple sets of records or books on continuity programs.

Candlelite has done well with its six record set, "The Elvis Presley Story," which it offered for $24.99 on credit terms at $5.99 per month via its direct mail solicitation.

■ To be sure, records still do well on television, but profits are not on the rise. "Records have worked on tv and radio for 25 years because they're a good value," V & R's Lindeman explains.

Record prices were one of the lowest increase items of the inflationary '70s, according to Mr. Catlan of K-Tel. But because of the fierce competitiveness of the business and reduced demand, manufacturers and distributors are being strangled by a cost-price squeeze.

It's difficult to explain why. It may be because the No. 1 selling albums are selling for the lowest prices in order to encourage traffic into retail stores. Consequently, those who sell via television must be ready to offer similar or lower prices to stay afloat. In the face of rising television costs and cost of materials, the profit margin continues to grow slimmer.

This is yet one more reason why tv direct response selling may soon take a backseat to the growing mail order business. Many of those who sell on television enclose catalogs of their merchandise along with the order. It is a system which attracts repeat business and it's also one which technically already puts these companies into the mail order business and moves them further away from television.

■ Another way direct marketers generate additional income is by selling their excess inventory at reduced rates to stores. Brookville, for example, sold a body-shaper exerciser gadget with ropes and pulleys on television. When the business finally fizzled out due to oversaturation by Brookville and its competitors, the exercisers were sold to retail outlets.

Popeil passed along its older stock in the same way, opting to purchase precious tv time to sell new, more attractive merchandise. However, contractual agreements with record companies prevent like sales of records. Many record companies grant sale rights to direct marketers for direct response type sales only. Retail sales often are taboo.

Over-all, caution and planning are the current watchwords of the business. Adventurous businessmen willing to take a gamble on a potentially hot item are giving way to careful analysis and strategy.

K-Tel's Imperial House, for example, has its direct marketing sales worked out to near-scientific perfection. By analyzing each buy, it develops a separate format for each item it wishes to sell, including when to run the commercials, how long, and what types of ads to prepare.

■ Other companies have made it a standard practice to test market a record before advertising it on nationwide television. V & R is currently test marketing a John Denver 'Greatest Hits' collection. Because the top sellers on tv are oldies and country and western records, selling a current artist on the air is somewhat of a gamble. The risk can be minimized by test marketing.

Despite careful planning, however, direct response, like any other business, can be unpredictable. No one seems to have the secret formula, although one company, the Sessions division of Audio Research in Chicago seems to have hit on something it doesn't wish to share with the rest of the world. Committed to maintaining a low profile, Sessions, one of the most successful sellers of oldies, refuses to give out any information whatsoever about its business.

In a business where many come and go, the candidness of two successful companies stands out. "We've been exceptional because we've been, I guess, lucky," says Wes Wood of Candlelite. Don Mundo of Lakeshore Music says, "The secret to success in this business? Luck and knowing the marketplace." In that order?

# Where to Turn When Post Office Doesn't Deliver

**BY MARGIE PRITZKER**

CHICAGO—Is the high cost of postage causing direct marketers to seek alternate methods of delivery? What are the alternatives and what is the environment in which they operate?

There are many private, or alternate, delivery companies. The one characteristic they all have in common is that they are privately owned rather than government owned.

These companies can be divided into three general types. There are saturation delivery companies which deliver circulars and flyers to consumer homes. They employ as delivery people parttime workers, many of whom are housewives and students.

Second, there are cargo and package delivery companies, such as United Parcel Service or companies specializing in air freight.

Finally, there are selective, or target, delivery companies which deliver magazines, books and other items to specific address consumer homes. These companies also employ parttime delivery people from the secondary labor force.

Because of the complexity of the subject, only the private delivery of such direct marketing items as catalogs, books and the Carol Wright pieces from Donnelley Marketing will be examined.

What is causing direct marketers to seek other methods of delivery? Frank M. Magel, assistant vp, Book-of-the-Month Club (BOMC), said that the escalation of postal rates is the primary factor in seeking other methods of delivery.

"Our philosophy," he noted, "is that we will look at anyone who can deliver the books reliably for the least money."

Herbert Gertz, vp-government services, Donnelley Marketing, agrees that the broad concern is the cost of postage, either now or in the future. He said that a number of people are positioning themselves not so much for current savings, which may be close to a trade-off, but so that when the rates become threatening, "they will have a resource set up to jump."

Although most people believe that the cost of postage is a factor, some mentioned other reasons also. Dante Zacavish, vp-educational marketing, Direct Mail/Marketers Assn. (DMMA), described private delivery as a new medium.

■ He said that direct marketers as a group are creative, inventive and dynamic; thus, when a concept like private delivery comes along, "they stand back, look at it and say, 'Here's another form of direct distribution. Does it have economic power for me in terms of economic effectiveness and cost efficiency?' It's another way of bringing goods into the direct marketing channel."

John R. Sweeney Jr., president, National Assn. of Selective Distributors (NASD), agreed with Mr. Zacavish, adding, "Our basic contention in the association is that many of the selective marketing pieces that we're delivering are pieces that would not normally go through the mail. They are pieces that are designed, contrived and paid for based on a new marketing concept, a new medium.

"That's why, when you look at the statistics of the bulk third class mail, as the private distribution of books and records has grown, there has been very little decrease in the volume of the third class mail going through the U.S. Postal Service."

Although private delivery has been around for years in the form of saturation distribution, private delivery of books, records and similar items is a much more recent phenomenon. Companies range in size from small "ma and pa" operations working out of their garage to operations which are subsidiaries of large conglomerates, including H & R Block, Harte-Hanks Communications, Knight-Ridder Newspapers, Warner Communications and ARA Services.

■ High penetration and high density are commonly believed to be factors necessary to make the use of private delivery effective on a cost basis. Therefore, it is used mainly in metropolitan areas rather than rural. A number of private deliverers mentioned that this process of skimming off the most cost efficient areas for private delivery and leaving the less populated and rural areas for the Postal Service has caused the USPS considerable concern.

Cost savings, or the lack of them, vary to some extent according to the type of item being delivered and in what class it would be mailed through the Postal Service. Privately delivered books which would be mailed special fourth class have resulted in cost savings for BOMC and *Reader's Digest*.

Rita Wecker, deputy director-corporate distribution, *Reader's*

*Digest,* said that approximately 40,000 *Reader's Digest* Condensed Books are distributed five times a year by private deliverers. They are distributed in Los Angeles with Harte-Hanks Distribution; in Grand Rapids, with American Field Marketing, a subsidiary of Harte-Hanks, and in Boston with CMS, a subsidiary of Warner Communications.

Although Ms. Wecker did not release specific cost figures, she said that the rate paid to the private deliverer plus freight is less than the Postal Service cost. She added that the service and time frame provided by each is comparable.

■ Mr. Magel said that in 1969, the special fourth class rate was 12¢ for the first pound and 6¢ for each additional pound to send a book anywhere in the country. In July, 1979, the cost was 59¢ for the first pound, 22¢ for each additional pound through seven and 13¢ for each pound over seven.

BOMC, he said, ships approximately 30,000 book packages a day and that figure may reach 35,000 a day during the fall and early spring; the packages average just under three pounds. In a cost comparison, the freight charge to get the book package to the private delivery company must be added to the delivery charge paid to the private deliverer.

Considering these costs, Mr. Magel said in a speech before the National Postal Forum East in Niagara Falls, N.Y., in October, 1979, that BOMC, in its use of private delivery, was saving 28¢ a package in Michigan, 29¢ in Massachusetts and 46¢ in Pennsylvania.

"We've been using private delivery about two years," he said, "and I think we're going to continue with it. We think that it can be done and that it is a way of saving us money."

■ Direct marketers like Donnelley Marketing who use third class bulk when delivering through the

Postal Service are in a different situation. Donnelley's Carol Wright co-op is a syndicated mailing which they make six times a year, usually in the amount of 21,000,000 pieces.

Although Donnelley uses private delivery in selected areas, Mr. Gertz said, "The Postal Service did an excellent thing in stemming the incidence of that alternate flow when it introduced the carrier route discount. The basic charge for third class bulk is 8.4¢, but with the carrier route discount one can save 1.5¢, bringing the rate to 6.9¢, if one prepares the mail in a certain fashion and sorts it out by carrier route. That was a welcome relief," Mr. Gertz added, "and certainly for us has slowed and limited our interest in moving toward private delivery."

Commenting on the subject of private delivery for catalogs, John Engle, catalog distribution manager, Sears, Roebuck & Co., said that it was tested several years ago for some of their supplements. When the cost of trucking the supplements to the private deliverer was added to the delivery cost, he said, "It was pretty much of a washout."

According to Richard Patton, advertising vp, Aldens, the company distributes 60,000,000 catalogs a year, 10,000,000 of which are fourth class and the rest are third class. It, too, tested private delivery for its catalogs, but is no longer using it, he said, because its concentrations were not high enough, costs were more than using the Postal Service and the incidence of nondelivery increased.

The advantages and disadvantages of private delivery are carefully weighed by direct marketers who are considering alternatives. Advantages include cost savings in some cases, generally faster delivery, the ability to target a specific date or pair of dates for delivery, the possibility of enclosing other advertising material in the package at no extra cost and the use of what some term "a new medium."

Disadvantages include freight and shipping difficulties and costs; no national network; lack of quality control in many cases and a limited choice of markets.

Mr. Sweeney said, "The biggest problem we have is that we do not have a security system like the Postal Service. We have to compete with the Postal Service and not on equitable or fair ground." In addition to the USPS monopoly on delivery of letters, only mail delivered by the Postal Service can be deposited in a mailbox.

In his October speech, Mr. Magel said that reliability is sometimes a problem. "How about the guy who thinks he'd like to make some extra money delivering your packages, but finds, after the first day, he doesn't like the work and puts the rest of your books down in his basement."

■ In 1978, in response to the competition provided by private delivery companies and in an attempt to make the mails more attractive, the Postal Service formed the Alternate Delivery Task Force. It was composed of a number of teams, each cochaired by a postal official and an industry representative.

Bob Inhofe, director of distribution, Meredith Corp., was the cochairman of the Alternate Delivery Market Analysis team. He said the teams convened periodically and that work went on in a fairly formal way for about a year.

■ "By the time the Task Force formally concluded work," he said, "40 or 50 suggestions had been presented and 12 or 13 had been implemented." He added that Postmaster General William F. Bolger is determined to consider the other suggestions and has indicated a willingness to keep the suggestion channels flowing.

Attorney Francis X. Lilly, of Bryan, Cave, McPheeters & McRoberts in Washington, D.C., represents the NASD. Commenting on the NASD's concern over what they consider to be the Postal

Service's attempts to expand its monopoly, he said, "What bothers us is that we believe it has the possibility, if it is successful, of saying anything can be a letter. All that would matter in making the distinction is how it is delivered."

■ If the growth in the recent past is an indication, the future for the private delivery industry looks promising. Figures provided by NASD indicate that in 1977, it had only nine members delivering approximately 5,688,000 pieces annually into 106 Zip code areas. In 1979, it had 70 members delivering 14,592,000 pieces into 270 Zip code areas. NASD projections for calendar year 1980 are that it will have 109 members delivering approximately 60,000,000 pieces annually into 2,244 Zip codes.

Looking to the future, Mr. Wright said that the more services private delivery companies can provide over and above selective and saturation distribution, the better off they will be.

■ Added Robert Marbut, president-ceo, Harte-Hanks Communications, "Regarding the future, I think a lot has to do with how postal rates go and how effective they are. I think a lot has to do with how well the distribution companies are able to develop the capability to do both target and selective saturation; in other words, delivering on a saturation basis but only to certain segments of the market.

"A lot will hinge on how effectively the companies will learn to put these two systems in place under the same management and get some benefits and economies by combining elements of the two systems."

# Columbia House—Profile of Success

## BY WALLY TOKARZ

NEW YORK—"The point I'm making," said Ben Ordover, "is that there is often the belief that to be successful in direct marketing you've got to have a product that isn't available anywhere else—that's really not true."

Mr. Ordover should know. He's president of Columbia House, a division of CBS/Columbia Group, one of four operating groups of CBS Inc.

And Columbia House and direct marketing are synonymous.

Among the mail order items offered by Columbia House are its continuous series of special interest books such as "The World of Automobiles" and "Make it Yourself" (a craft series).

■ The Needle Arts Society offers books on knitting, crocheting and needlepoint as well as supply kits. And, its House of Miniatures collectors series offers a line of miniature replicas of unassembled, American furniture of the 17th and 18th Centuries.

But the mainstay, which makes up approximately 75% of Columbia House's profits, is the music business. It is represented primarily by the Columbia Record & Tape Club.

The current club offer is 13 records or tapes for a penny, plus postage and handling. For that price the member makes a commitment to buy nine records or tapes over a three-year period at the regular club prices.

The CBS annual report for 1978 states that Columbia Record & Tape Club is the largest mail order distributor of recorded music in the world with a membership of more than 4,000,000. Its profits in '78 were $33,600,000 on revenues of $598,900,000 (AA, Sept. 6).

■ While many businesses, including the music business, experienced sales and profits slippages in 1979, Columbia House maintained its prosperity.

The reason, according to Mr. Ordover, is by "being very careful in where you market. We are successful even though the music industry itself had problems in '79. I think that to stay successful in any period, whether good or bad," he continued, "is to do your thing better than anybody else in direct marketing."

Others may dispute that claim, but the record is self-evident: Columbia Record & Tape Club is celebrating its 25th anniversary.

Looking at offers from major direct marketing companies, there are in many instances the very same products being sold at retail. Advertising, therefore, is the magnet to draw the customer.

"With us, and I think with any successful club, the focal point is the offer," said Mr. Ordover. "Essentially, advertising in direct marketing is almost always focused on an offer or proposition, a deal. What you're saying is that, from me to you, I offer you an unusually good opportunity.

■ "To back up that offer you must have a very good grouping of products to make sure that your club is

24

Among the offers made by direct marketing king Columbia House are "Make it Yourself" kits containing patterns for clothing and household knitted and crocheted items, as well as a deal on records and tapes. The well known club currently allows joining members the chance to receive 13 of either the records or the tapes for 1¢.

current and to make sure your offer is meaningful. The essence of our program is a wide variety of current products from many different musical labels. Our club represents 85% of the entire market."

Handling all of Columbia House's advertising is Wunderman, Ricotta & Kline, New York. *TV Guide,* with an eight-page insert, is by far the No. 1 medium used. Booklets for *Parade* and *Family Weekly* and preprints inserted into Sunday newspapers also are used heavily.

"We are trying to hit the widest possible audience effectively with a special unit at the lowest cost per thousand," said Mr. Ordover.

During 1978 nearly $20,000,000 was spent in measured media— $8,793,000 in magazines, $6,275,400 in newspaper supplements and $4,616,700 in spot tv (AA, Sept. 6). Mr. Ordover indicated that there is no effort to reduce advertising this year, but that they do want to make a more intelligent use of it. More television advertising will be used in support of print.

■ He also explained that many members do not rejoin after their membership expires. "There is a certain fatigue. They drop out. They don't continue like magazine subscribers because it's a vastly different kind of program. Remember, they get an upfront offer and then they have to buy a certain amount. They get somewhat tired of the discipline of club activity and some of them leave.

"So," added Mr. Ordover, "the need to do new prospecting is an ongoing fact in direct marketing. I know of very few direct marketing companies that don't need to have an aggressive, new membership program."

Aside from music, other Columbia House products, especially the special interest libraries, rely on direct mail advertising. "We can identify from a list the type of interest a person has, his past purchasing patterns, and then zero in on him in an advertising message

from that specific list," said Mr. Ordover.

With all the success Columbia House has experienced, Mr. Ordover is not being boastful when he talks about his competition. "You're always going against competition and that's healthy," he said. "We view it as being very necessary to make us do better and to fight harder for the customer. I don't know specifically of a competitor who has crippled us in any way."

■ But to assume that Columbia House has succeeded in all its attempts is far from the truth. All it touches does not turn to gold.

A record club in the United Kingdom and a beauty program in the U.S. in the early '70s were failures. The latter focused on importing beauty aids from other countries and was called Importa. The most beautiful cosmetics of a particular country would be imported and then offered in a kit.

"This went over like a lead balloon," said Mr. Ordover. "I think the basic premise was ridiculous. America, and perhaps France, produce the best beauty products in the world."

As for the U.K. record club, he stated that there was an operational problem of some magnitude. "You just simply can't work out of one country where you learn how to operate every facet of the business, particularly how to deal with customers and how to control credit and shipments, and walk into another country which has a vastly different social and economic phase. You may think it is similar, but it isn't. It takes you a while to begin to understand how to operate in that environment."

■ Along with the successes and failures also come surprises. Technology plays a major role in these.

"When tapes came into the industry in the late '60s they made a fantastic difference in the over-all response to music club ads," explained Mr. Ordover. "A curious fact is that tapes in direct market-ing represent a much bigger per-centage of the over-all units sold than they do at retail.

"Lp's are still, by far, the leading unit sellers in retail, which is not true in mail order. Tapes are very strong. The general opinion of the industry is that it's more difficult to display tapes in retail. They're much more susceptible to theft and so they're often put away in cabinets. But records are usually placed in racks which allow you to browse through them. Retailers are much more reluctant to openly dis-play tapes, especially the small cas-settes," Mr. Ordover said.

Technology also is a major factor for future Columbia House prod-ucts. One area where research and planning already has begun is videocassettes. However, certain questions must be answered be-fore further steps are taken.

■ "There are a lot of problems to sort out in the industry concerning machine compatibility," said Mr. Ordover. "And, you have clubs now that have rental approaches *vs.* clubs that have outright sale ap-proaches. You also have a lot of people running around doing a lot of licensing of movie products. But, we do feel that there is a future for them with us.

"I'd say that in the next several years Columbia House will broaden its base. We certainly will concentrate on music and all its as-pects in terms of video music and video entertainment. We think sound and any aspect of sound is very directly related to our market.

"As to other products," Mr. Or-dover continued, "I think what is really required of us is to try to de-tect and to anticipate what the pop-ulation wants, and then to relate this to meaningful direct market-ing where you can do it by conven-ience, where you can give people a choice, save them time and zero into their interests. The one thing we try to avoid are fads."

■ Ben Ordover has worked in di-rect marketing for 20 years. He joined Columbia House as vp of marketing in 1972. In 1978 he be-came executive vp and was named president last June. His career has taught him that "the direct market-ing world provides a very trying discipline. It's one where you learn quickly whether something works or doesn't.

"I think people tend to view ad-vertising by how pretty it is. This is a great mistake. It comes from the consumer world of advertising. They tend to look at an ad and if it's pretty or if it's cute, it's good. There is nothing further from the truth.

"None of those factors has any-thing to do with the success," said Mr. Ordover. "We all like to do pretty things because they easily persuade people that that's the best thing, but I think they're su-perficial.

"Direct marketing is a hard disci-pline, and it's a sales discipline in that the ad itself is the salesman. You never are going to get another chance. It requires a whole differ-ent approach to understand it and too often it is judged by standards that have nothing to do with what it is."

# Collectibles — A New Market

**BY DONN PEARLMAN**

CHICAGO—Whether the item be Elvis Presley plates or limited edition silver medals, collectibles is an area that seems perfectly to lend itself to direct marketing sales techniques.

Two of the most successful direct marketing companies in collectibles are the Franklin Mint of Franklin Center, Pa. and First Coin Investors (FCI) of Albertson, N.Y.

Both companies report multi-million-dollar sales and their customers the past decade can reap healthy profits, too, either from the boom in rare coins and stamps, the astounding increases in silver bullion prices or a combination of both.

■ The Franklin Mint backs up its worldwide mailing list solicitations with 2,000,000 active collectors with advertising schedules in daily newspapers, such specialty journals and "prestige publications" as *National Geographic* and *Smithsonian,* according to a FM representative.

"Our collectors generally are more affluent, urban rather than rural, relatively mature and have significantly more education than the average person," he explained.

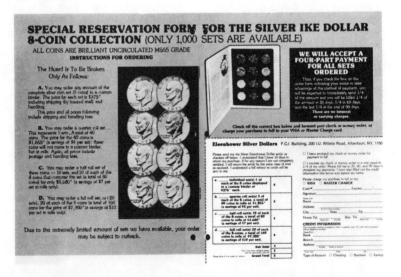

First Collectors Inc. devoted entire issue of its magazine to Eisenhower silver dollars, including full page spread with coupon.

Direct mail offerings from the Franklin Mint are works of art in themselves—glossy, often four-color illustration presentations with detailed, descriptive narrative on the items offered. Considerable attention and adjectives are devoted to the creativity and beauty of the items.

The FM product line is varied and has undergone a tremendous change the past four years. A product mix that had been 80% medallic and numismatic (coins) is now only 20% medallic and numismatic.

There are 150 to 200 product offerings a year for sculptures, etchings, fine books and porcelain pieces. A recent item aimed at big ticket order generating is a replica of a 1765 Townsend Chippendale desk. The original, in a U.S. State Department diplomatic reception room, is valued at $250,000 and is not for sale.

The FM re-creation is for sale at $4,800, part of the new Franklin Heirloom Furniture line.

"The '60 Minutes' piece hurt us," admits the FM representative, referring to a 1978 critical report by CBS News correspondent Morley Safer. The report hammered away at the Franklin Mint's alleged luring of investment-oriented customers by use of such phrases as "sterling silver limited editions" and "limited quantities."

In the tv program Safer was filmed buying a FM silver medal at one coin store, then selling it for a loss at another. Several owners of FM products were interviewed about their failure to make a profit or come close to breaking even on their extensive purchases.

"If you were to go into Tiffany's and buy a silver service, then turn around and take it to Cartier's, they certainly wouldn't offer you the retail price," the FM representative reasoned. "Why should they?"

If Mr. Safer conducted the same medallion buying and selling experiment at Manhattan coin shops today he would get the same results. One usually fails to make a quick profit purchasing nearly anything at retail and immediately selling it at wholesale.

His interviewees who unhappily attempted to dispose of their FM holdings, however, should be smiling today if they go to sell. Silver prices have tripled since the "60 Minutes" report was aired.

■ "After that broadcast, a number of our customers cancelled their subscriptions," the FM representative recalled. "Some of them were stampeded by the tv show to sell their collections, which was a very unwise decision."

Are Franklin Mint products worth the money? It depends on what you seek. Quality workmanship is a FM standard. Many buyers prominently display their collectibles. Even FM products designed for "hoarding" are showcase material.

For example, its new quarter, one-half oz. and one-oz. gold bullion "coins" (positioned in the marketplace as "the American alternative" as they are produced with U.S. gold) are exquisitely designed by former U.S. Mint engraver Gilroy Roberts.

But are FM's previous series of beautiful medals and art bars "overpriced junk" as some critics claim?

Beauty is in the eye of the beholder; bullion is in the heart of the investor.

■ In 1970, FM began producing a series of 200 sterling silver medals depicting events in the history of the U.S. The medals were issued to mail order subscribers at the rate of two per month at a cost of $9.75 each.

Also in 1970, the New York spot silver prices peaked at $1.93 an ounce. The FM history medals weigh 1.3 oz. each.

One subscriber who paid $1,950 for the entire history set issued over an eight-year period recently sold his collection to a Chicago coin dealer for $3,460. The tremendous jump in silver prices turned his medallic art collection into a bullion investment. For every $9.75 he spent, it yielded $18.20.

(Now if he originally spent that $9.75 on a choice brilliant uncirculated silver dollar minted in New

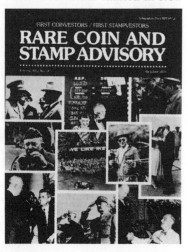

FIRST COINVESTORS / FIRST STAMPVESTORS

RARE COIN AND STAMP ADVISORY

**Front cover of FCI's "Advisory" devoted to Eisenhower silver dollars featured a collage of photos spanning his war and presidential careers.**

Orleans in 1879, he would have a $300 return, but that's just the author's numismatic bias showing.)

"Nearly everyone who bought Franklin Mint items is a winner today," the coin dealer noted. "I think the medals are things of beauty, you could keep them in the family to enjoy for 100 years, but many people are selling them now because of the high intrinsic value, the bullion value."

The collecting-for-collecting's sake aspect is stressed in current FM direct marketing materials. Denying the "60 Minutes" allegations, the FM representative was emphatic: "With the exception of one product, the gold bullion pieces, we have never oriented any of our products to the investor or said anything had an investment potential."

A few early FM items, produced in rather small quantities by today's "limited issue" standards, command collector premiums.

Franklin Mint's earnings picture has improved since the CBS encounter. Net profits for the first nine months of 1979 were $7,400,000 compared to $5,400,000 the previous year. FM has opened two retail outlets (suburban Detroit and Washington, D.C.) and recently acquired Eastern Mountain Sports, a retail store chain and direct mail sporting goods company.

A collecting-for-investing's sake approach is emphasized by First Coin Investors of Albertson, N.Y. The 12-year-old company is riding high on the growing wave of coin and stamp buying by investors who have big hopes but little knowledge about this field of collectibles.

■ "Our potential market is not only those people who know about rising values of rare coins and stamps, but people who have not been happy or satisfied with other investments, maybe mutual funds or the stock market," explained FCI vp-sales Marvin Schaffer.

"They want to branch out. They don't know about rare stamp and coin investment potential, only the kids' buying 5¢ and 10¢ items as a hobby. And, if they have heard about it, they don't know how to go about it."

FCI distributes a monthly "Rare Coin and Stamp Advisory" to a regular mailing list of more than 25,000 potential customers. Additional special offer mailings are sent every 4 to 6 weeks and there is emphasis on regular, continuing-purchase programs such as "Rare Gold Management," the "U.S. Silver Dollar Society," and the "U.S. Type Coin Program" where participants can receive monthly shipments according to their previously specified cost limits.

An integral part of the total sales effort is the follow-up telephone call. All FCI order form applications request both the customer's home and work telephone numbers. "Phone contact goes hand-in-glove with our mailings," stressed Jack Lee, exec vp-marketing. "It is very important."

FCI account execs try to establish a one-to-one relationship with clients as a supplement to the mailings. The personal contact not only boosts sales, it corrects misconceptions.

■ "We tell people if they are not in a position to put something away for four or five years, then stamps and coins are not for them. We turn away a lot of business from people looking to double their money in six months," Mr. Schaffer revealed.

A look at FCI's balance sheet indicates many other people are not dissuaded. The company had 1978 net sales of $6,500,000 compared to $5,700,000 the year before.

Net income rose to $250,566 in 1978. Figures for 1979, although not yet available, are expected to show continued very strong growth.

"We're the largest publicly held company specifically involved in rare stamp and coin investments," Mr. Lee proudly pointed out.

FCI's monthly "Advisory" is a well researched, two-dozen page thesis on the ravages of inflation and the upwardly mobile financial history of selected coin and stamp items being offered for sale. Each specific offering usually consists of two or more pages of illustrated sales pitch "personalized" with the name and photograph of an FCI executive or consultant.

The company shuns what one official called "tulip crazes" and "manufactured limited edition rarities from private mints," instead concentrating on selected coins and stamps with solid investment potential.

■ The front cover of a recent "Advisory," touting the investment potential of eight different Eisenhower $1 coins, had 10 photographs of Dwight David Eisenho-

wer at various military and political stages of his life. Eight more similar photos covered an inside page, six others on the back cover.

All eight coins were also pictured (although to the layman they may appear exactly alike except for different dates) and their history outlined. In all, 13 of the "Advisory's" 24 pages were devoted to the "I Like Ike" dollars campaign.

■ The bottom line: The special eight-coin set in a custom holder was priced at $375 with modest discounts for orders of 5, 10, or 20 sets. However, the collector/-investor with some basic numismatic knowledge and a little time to shop could easily assemble from local or mail-order coin dealers the same coin set (minus FCI's custom holder) for only $275 to $300 per set.

■ Is FCI "charging too much" for its mail order merchandise?

"When you buy stocks and bonds through a broker you pay a commission . . . so why should you object to a similar charge on the part of FCI in the form of a higher price for a coin?" writes A. George Mallis, an acknowledged expert on U.S. silver dollars and one of FCI's 80 staff members and consultants.

His statement is included in the Eisenhower issue "Advisory" as part of an explanation of why the company does not sell "cheap" coins or stamps.

"We guarantee quality," Mr. Schaffer added in a recent conversation. "We offer a service with a guaranteed quality product in a field where unfortunately there are people who take advantage of a customer's lack of knowledge," he emphasized, referring to the problems of proper grading—the correct description of the amount or lack of wear on a coin's surface. Grading is a tremendous factor in the value of most coins. Stamps, too.

Even customers paying "high"

prices can be winners if they buy accurately graded merchandise. In 1976, FCI advertised and sold sets of brilliant uncirculated 1948 to 1963 Franklin half-dollars for $395 per set. Two years later, when an astute collector/investor could buy a similar 35-coin set for about $400, FCI was quickly selling out its second Franklin half-dollar offering with a direct mail price of $515.

■ Today those same sets wholesale for about $900 each.

Several problems confront FCI's direct marketing approach. One is the company's ability to stock enough of any specific item or sets to meet customer demand. Many offerings are quickly sold out. Another problem is fighting rapidly fluctuating coin, stamp and bullion markets.

A special mailing to enroll subscribers in a rare coin purchase program (at predetermined monthly customer costs of between $50 and $750) included an introductory offer to buy a roll of common date 90% silver dimes at only $39.

■ By the time the special mailing was packaged with one free silver dime enclosed, shipped, and received, the intrinsic bullion value of the dime roll was $42.50 (with each silver dime worth 85¢).

Now, four months later, the bullion value is around $60 per roll.

Multiply that cost overrun headache by a mailing list in excess of 25,000 and it is easy to understand why FCI attempted to substitute the dime rolls with less costly "rare" silver dollars to fill the orders.

FCI President Stanley Apfelbaum wrote to customers, "I feel terrible. . . . I hope that this [the substitute and lower value merchandise] will serve to ameliorate my embarrassment." He put most of the blame, not on the unexpected sharp increase in bullion prices, but on the problems of "the lousy delivery of the mails."

Customers returning the unordered silver dollars and insisting on the delivery of the dimes received the dimes along with a check for their postage and a gracious note from Mr. Apfelbaum offering immediately to buy back the $39 roll for $55.

The FCI "Rare Coin and Stamp Advisory" used to carry a (seldom paid) subscription price of $17.50 per year. To attract subscribers for the mailing list, FCI would offer a "free subscription" if new customers purchased a two-peso Mexican coin—for only $17.50.

With gold in excess of $365 an ounce there is more than $17.50 worth of gold in the two-peso coin. Now FCI's print ads in various financial and numismatic publications make the same gold coin/free subscription offer, but the current price is $22.50. When gold goes over the next breakeven point of $455, FCI probably will have to again increase its free subscription price.

■ "Better Than Gold?" reads the bold teaser on the mailing envelope of the Low-Mintage Coin Club of Montpelier, Vt., a direct mail coin investment organization that sells foreign coins with mintages of under 3,000.

An introductory four-page letter highlights amazing increases in values for their previous offerings and a four-color, almost poster-size told-out provides details of present sale items ranging in price from $28 for an official eight-piece mint set of 1975 Swiss coins to $2,150 for the four 1977 gold coins produced by the Isle of Man. Postage is extra.

Free bonus gifts—a coin holder album, investment guide and back issues of the club's monthly reports—also are offered if the customer's first order and membership application are sent within 15 days.

Customers have 90 days to cancel their membership and return the coins for a full refund, but may keep the bonus gifts "worth over $20."

Are low-mintage coins "better than gold?" as the club's direct mail letter concludes?

Yes and no.

■ Just because you are buying a properly graded, authentic coin of which very few were produced does not mean it will skyrocket in value, bullion fluctuations notwithstanding.

Supply of the low-mintage coins may be quite limited, but so is the present demand among most collectors and investors compared to, for example, the 1941 to 1963 half dollars. If the Low-Mintage Coin Club continues to successfully promote membership and increase purchase demands through its direct marketing approach, maybe that $28 coin set from Switzerland may one day cost the same as the $2,150 Isle of Man gold coin set.

Whether it will be worth the price remains to be seen.

# Impact on Insurance Selling

## BY JOHN FLIEDER

CHICAGO—Changes in life style have produced a tremendous impact on insurance marketing. With the increased mobility of the country's population, many insurance buyers become "disconnected" from their local agents. This results in people looking more to continuity with the company from which they buy rather than to continuity with a particular agent.

Companies recognize this, and thus today, virtually every insurance company uses the mail to maintain policyholder contact as well as to sell group and association plans in addition to individual business.

And many of the most successful agents use the mail to develop inquiries, qualify prospects and follow-up on established clients.

Recent consumer studies clearly document the tremendous growth of the mail order segment of marketing programs for an increasingly wide variety of products and services. Direct mail in combination with personal contact, with either being the dominant distribution system, has become a recognized marketing strategy. This follows from increasingly significant shifts in consumer buying patterns, including the purchase and

servicing of life, health, accident and casualty insurance.

- The positive effects of various consumer movements as well as efforts of the Direct Mail/Marketing Assn. have brought the mail order business to the point where consumer confidence in products and services offered by mail is at an all-time high and rising.

To respond most effectively to the needs of the consumer with direct mail, the insurance industry's marketing activities have become more sophisticated. We find ourselves segmenting the vast total marketplace into smaller and more homogeneous units as we seek to maximize efficiency. Not one of us in the entire insurance industry can afford to call on everyone, either by mail or in person.

- In the beginning, market segmentation in the insurance industry was geographic and demographic. Attention was focused on rural areas, where agent representation was sparse. Most recently, this segmentation has been more psychographic, too—by habits, attitudes, life styles and behavior patterns of consumers, wherever they are to be found.

A major psychographic trend follows from changing family patterns with more married women entering the work force. Insurance protection for both wage-earning spouses as well as for single heads of households has become more recognized as an economic necessity than ever before.

*John Flieder is assistant vp-marketing, Allstate Insurance Co., Chicago, and chairman, Direct Marketing Insurance Council.*

According to Joseph Cooper, J. C. Penney Life Insurance Co., many companies are now finding that more than half of the policies being sold by mail are being bought to cover women; as more and more women are heading households, they are purchasing more insurance.

The American Council of Life Insurance states that the average amount of coverage represented by policies purchased for women rose 86% from 1972 to 1977, and women bought 29% of new policies in 1977, up from 24% in 1972.

Working members of households usually are limited in the time they have available for shopping for goods and services. With more wives and singles working in addition to their home and family responsibilities, and with frequent family moves breaking down ties to agents, the time-saving and convenience of buying reliable goods and services by mail, including insurance, becomes more appealing.

The convenience of reliable products offered by mail is attractive to another growing segment of the insurance market. With the extended longevity of our population, the senior members of our society are becoming a larger and larger segment of the direct marketed insurance marketplace.

■ About 10% of the U.S. population is 65 years and older. For this group, direct marketing is particularly suited as a distribution alternative for the kinds of coverage they need most.

The senior citizen especially appreciates the ease and convenience of shopping by mail. Older persons often view mailed literature as information about products and services they cannot seek out on their own. They read and study product information at their leisure, and make their decisions in their own time.

Martin Baier, committee member of Direct Marketing Insurance Council and vp-marketing, Old

American Insurance Co., cites results of research in this area done by his company: "There is an apparent need of the older person for stimulation from the world around him, together with an increased need for contact with other people. As the physical vitality and the intellectual vigor of the elderly person diminishes, he experiences greater need for vicarious satisfactions and stimulations.

"Reading materials [including direct mail], along with television and radio, provide him contact with others, particularly if these materials report news of some type."

■ A number of years ago, most insurance companies were ignoring the 65-plus age segment. Many still do today. We are told that as we grow older, life insurance, for example, becomes more difficult for us to obtain. It becomes unprofitable for many insurance companies to sell policies to this age bracket. Where can they get coverage? The direct marketers of insurance have tailored policies for these people.

Each year, those who are over 65 learn that they are obliged to pay more and more for the services that are not covered by Social Security and Medicare.

For example, social security funeral benefits have remained the same for 20 years, yet we all know that the cost of dying has gone up considerably during those years. So the supplemental coverages provided by direct marketing insurance companies are a necessity.

■ For the estate planning and the business market, the agents' professional function will continue to be essential. Personal attention will remain indispensable in this segment of the market.

But for many segments of the market, insurance by mail may be the only economically sound mechanism for offering simple protection to the many consumers who do not command an agent's attention, especially as more market segments are identified through marketing techniques for efficient direct mail merchandising.

■ The 1975-76 Life Insurance Marketing & Research Assn. research report, "The Opportunity to Buy," showed that although there was a 7% increase in the number of households that actually purchased insurance, only 35% of all U.S. households had some contact with the agency system. That represents a drop from 39% in 1967, when a previous study was done. So, for about two-thirds of all American households, buying through the mail may be the only means of buying insurance, simply because agents aren't available or interested in them.

■ Direct marketing of all insurance utilizes a time-honored mode of agent selling—that is, making contact with prospects by means of mailed announcements, newsletters and sometimes even offers of premiums or gifts. What is new in our mode of selling is that we also ask for the order by mail.

Direct-marketed insurance doesn't replace the agent. It goes where agents don't go, for whatever reason.

# Marketing the "Good Stuff"—13-30 Corp. Case History

NASHVILLE—What advertiser could resist this kind of offer: A medium that would reach more than a million young, impressionable buyers.

Not only would it reach them, but would offer them a sample of a product when they needed it and were likely to try it immediately. Coupled with this, there would be strict surveys and tests to measure product awareness and use both before distributing the sample and again after 90 days.

Sound like something in a dream?

■ If it is a dream, then 13-30 Corp. is riding in the clouds. The youth-oriented company, which publishes a number of magazines, also has a marketing program called Good Stuff.

Essentially, 13-30 packs an average of 16 nationally-known products plus a variety of test items into a colorful box labeled Good Stuff.

Overseen by 13-30 representatives, the boxes are distributed to 1,050,000 incoming college students—mainly freshmen—each fall. The sample boxes reach dormitory students on 800 campuses. Of the nation's 1,600,000 college students living in dorms, about 63% get a Good Stuff box.

At the time of distribution, about 2,400 students respond to a prod-uct survey handed out by 13-30 reps. In 90 days, 13-30 circulates the same survey to different students in the dorm to measure current usage, most recent usage and intent to purchase factors for each product included in the sampler.

In two years, the number of participants in the Good Stuff program has increased from nine to 21. Robert Hanggi, director of sampling programs for 13-30, says there is room for more products in the Good Stuff box, and it will expand in coming years.

■ By their support of Good Stuff and their continuing interest in the program, manufacturers have shown their pleasure with the results. "It isn't a cheap program, what with a million samples and 13-30's fees," said one executive from a company that participates in the program. "But the results we get are great."

Oil of Olay (Richardson-Merrell Co.) has enjoyed some of the most dramatic success because of its participation. Originally targeting its moisturizing product at a 35-plus female market, the company's execs decided to test the 18 to 34 market.

Among the tests was inclusion in Good Stuff boxes. 13-30's surveys showed that many of the college women who tried the sample purchased the product and became regular users. "We have discovered that Oil of Olay does have a place in the 18 to 34 market," said a company representative.

A 1978 survey of students who received the Good Stuff packages and a survey of local stores showed sales of the products included in Good Stuff increased 119% in the campus-area shops.

■ Although 13-30 Corp. has found a successful formula, it was not luck. "It came to us (in 1976) that if we could segment and control our distribution, college dorms would be the perfect target for such a marketing plan," siad Mr. Hanggi. "We can literally put a good product where they live and then measure the results."

But 13-30 took many precautions to assure participating companies that it would maintain strict control over all phases of the program. Previous distribution programs with similar goals had failed because of inefficiency and occasional fraud.

The company instituted a number of quality controls, including fulltime field account execs, nonstudent campus representatives, contracts with each university housing authority, and annual assembly warehouse audit by Arthur Andersen Co. to ensure each box has the proper samples, computerized tracking capabilities, an independent distribution audit by Gilbert Youth Research and a money-back guarantee to manufacturers if 13-30 does not reach at least 90% of its projected distribution figure.

"One of the very attractive aspects of this program is that the group [13-30] is very buttoned up," said one manufacturer representative. "They have a lot of check points throughout the system—a lot of safeguards."

While manufacturers demand a lot of 13-30, the company also has many requirements before it will include a product in its Good Stuff package. "Will it appeal to a younger market?" asked Mr. Hanggi. "Is it a practical and usable product? Is it a quality product? We ask those questions and do a lot of testing. We also don't accept products that university officials might not appreciate. We're really their guests on campus, so we play by their rules."

■ As another of its marketing services, 13-30 provides potential clients with market research. Mr. Hanggi says that in the future, 13-

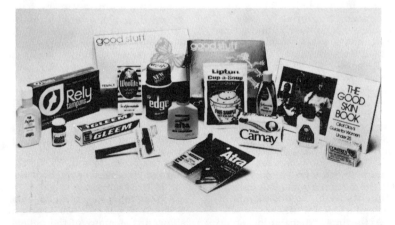

**For today's college student, 13-30 provides a box filled with personal care products that he or she can sample.**

30 will likely launch a similar marketing program for newlyweds, new parents and other easily identifiable markets. The company expects to use its publications— *Esquire, The Graduate, New Marriage, 18 Almanac, Nutshell* and others to find those target audiences.

13-30 began when college students Christopher Whittle and Phillip Moffitt decided to start a magazine aimed at college students. *Nutshell* has grown into the nation's largest circulation college magazine with a circulation of 1,200,000 (3,000,000 readers).

# Fighting the Alligators—Ohio Printing Case History

DAYTON, O.—The image of the Ohio Printing Co. was something less than sterling.

The company's customers knew it did good printing work at a fair price. It was good when it came to providing advice on projects and also offered speedy service. But the Ohio Printing Co. had no pizzaz.

An informal telephone survey conducted by the company of a selected group of 40 print buyers in the Dayton area showed that Ohio Printing ranked last among seven major printers in most-mentioned and the print buyers could not associate an image with Ohio Printing.

Jay Meiselman, vp of Ohio Printing, decided to establish a marketing approach. One of the first moves was to hire Ronald Ivanoff, an account exec with Needham, Harper & Steers in Dayton. Mr. Ivanoff became the marketing/communications director for the company.

■ "I almost ran from the job at first," says Mr. Ivanoff. "Working for a printing company didn't sound like a thriller."

But as he began to work with the company, he says he realized there was great potential for marketing. "Printers have traditionally not been into marketing," he says. "I tried to think how we could create an image for ourselves."

In an after-hours session, the Ohio Printing staff members sat down and talked about what they felt were the most important aspects of their work. Most often, the staff and sales people said the service they offered was a major selling point.

■ The company decided to market its service—speed, the ability to help print buyers reduce the pressures and hassles that come with their jobs. "There are a lot of printers who do work as good as ours," says Mr. Ivanoff. "And we weren't going to compete by undercutting prices. It seemed logical to impress potential clients that we could offer them better service.

■ To pull the promotion together, Ohio Printing needed an image

40

and a slogan. Mr. Ivanoff had used a saying for years. He sharpened it up and it came out like this: "The objective of all dedicated employes should be to thoroughly analyze all situations, anticipate all problems prior to their occurrence, and have answers for these problems when called upon. However . . .

"When you are up to your ears in alligators, it is difficult to remind yourself your initial objective was to drain the swamp. The Ohio Printing Co. We make the alligators go away."

The company used slogans and a stylized alligator sketch to emphasize to print buyers that Ohio Printing offered its skilled service to make their alligators go away and make their lives easier.

- Ohio Printing used three separate direct mail pieces and a magazine advertisement. The company rented a list of about 5,000 prospects in the Ohio area. Each mailing met a specific objective.

They first positioned Ohio Printing as a service-minded company and invited recipients to request a visit from an Ohio Printing salesman. The second mailing promoted the firm's five-color press. The third included a reply card and again emphasized the company's expertise in specialty areas. Each mailer invited print buyers to write for a color brochure, and alligator poster and note pads with Ohio Printing's name on them.

- After the nine-month campaign, the company conducted a survey of 40 different print buyers. The firm had moved from seventh (last) to third most-mentioned printer and from last in advertising awareness among print buyers to first.

As a result, sales increased dramatically and the company added more than a dozen new customers.

# Common Mistakes to Avoid

BY C. JAMES KEIL

PITTSBURGH—Direct marketing is no longer the exclusive tool of the entrepreneur or the mail order house. More and more advertisers are using direct response to help achieve their over-all objectives because they have discovered that it not only generates interest and awareness, but that direct marketing also can close the sale.

The increasing popularity of direct marketing has led to some growing pains, however—errors in judgment or strategy. Ten of the most common mistakes follow, for all direct marketers to take note and beware.

**1. Not segmenting the audience.** Each product is especially suitable for a specific audience. This target audience must be identified before anything else. The target audience will help determine the marketing and creative aspects of the program. Without a well defined and specific target audience, a direct marketing program becomes a blind effort.

**2. Assuming that testing one medium is enough.** Direct response advertising can be developed for use in all media, including direct mail, broadcast and space. A program may be appropriate for one or all media. But simply testing one doesn't tell you that the others necessarily will or will not work.

---

*C. James Keil is vp, Ketchum MacLeod and Grove, Pittsburgh.*

**3. Selecting the wrong media.** All of the strengths and weaknesses of the various media have to be taken into consideration before deciding on the proper one(s) for any one given program. In the case of direct mail, this can be as simple as selecting the proper lists. If you are selling something that is very complicated and/or very expensive, it doesn't make sense to try to sell it directly via space or broadcast. But you can use space or broadcast to generate leads that can later be converted to sales via direct mail.

**4. Using improper coding or failing to record results.** These are simple but important points that all too often are forgotten. The advertiser must be able to determine which ad or package in which media works best. This can be accomplished only with proper coding. Some advertisers will know how much they sold by daily cash receipts, but they will know little, if anything else, unless proper coding is used.

**5. Neglecting to plan in advance how to handle orders once they come in.** The majority of the effort and attention of a direct marketing campaign is usually given to the development of the advertising. But in direct marketing, it is important for the advertiser to be able to handle incoming orders efficiently and quickly. And to have an inventory control process that will notify him when to reorder products before they are out of stock.

**6. Proclaiming that long copy is not read.** Many advertisers work with an agency or a free lance copywriter to develop the creative form. Then the advertiser decides that the submitted copy is too long and nobody will read it. All direct marketing is based on testing. Every direct marketer can tell you that long copy is more effective than short copy—provided that both sets of copy are equally well written. It is important to remember that a direct marketer writes copy as long as necessary in order to effect a sale.

**7. Cutting corners on creative.** A decision can be made arbitrarily to go with four-color, two-color or b&w when, in fact, a coordinated representation of the product is needed to make the sale. Some advertisers will spend a lot of money on a brochure and then try to scrimp and save by using lower quality paper for the letter and envelope.

If full color is necessary to depict the product or support the message, then that decision should stand. It should not be changed for cost reasons.

If the creative decision is sound, you have a greater chance of showing more profit in the long run by coming up with a winning package rather than cutting corners to save a few dollars in the production.

**8. Attempting to cover all costs when evaluating the success/-failure of a program.** When developing direct marketing programs, there are going to be certain up front costs for mechanicals, plates, agency costs, etc. If an attempt is made to recoup these in the initial tests, the potential of the test to succeed becomes highly unlikely. These costs should be considered nonvariable costs. Only the variable costs (i.e., the cost of media, printing, the product and its fulfillment) should be considered costs to be recouped. The up front, nonvariable costs can be accounted for over the entire life of the program.

**9. Not allocating enough time to a program.** Two factors must be considered when planning a direct marketing program—lead time and response time. In direct mail, mailing and production time must be incorporated into the schedule before determining a drop rate. In space and broadcast, lead time and air time must be kept in mind. Once the program starts, be sure to allow enough time for orders to come in before analyzing the results determining the success/failure of the entire program.

**10. Forgetting that testing is the basis of direct marketing.** Any initial direct marketing packages are merely tests. The purpose of these packages is to learn whether or not the product or service can be sold via direct marketing and how it can be sold in the best and most efficient manner. Although parts of the test may not be successful, you will generally learn one or two basic items that can further expand for an improved program next time. Testing must continue, constantly seeking improvements, in order to build a successful direct marketing program.

Direct response advertising is now being used to sell thousands of products and services to virtually all markets. It has become the fastest growing method of advertising today. Let's try to make it the most nearly foolproof, too, by avoiding mistakes like these.

# Catalogs Are Booming

DALLAS—There is no doubt about it, the mail order catalog business is booming. Even the U.S. Postal Service is promoting it in the form of a bumper sticker that reads: Save gas, shop by mail.

The catalog business can be traced as far back as 1872, when Aaron Montgomery Ward decided he could reach midwestern farmers, who lived miles from any available shopping, through his catalogs.

Today, an estimated $87 billion worth of goods and services are purchased through direct mail. In 1978, there were about 85,000,000 catalogs in the mailstream representing about 8,000 companies. Over the past 10 years, the industry has nearly quadrupled.

Donna Sweeney, public relations director of the Direct Mail Marketing Assn., said that to trace the recent rise in catalog sales you need to go back about 12 years to the late '60s.

"There were two main factors that triggered the industry. With the advent of the computer, direct marketers were now able to sit back and identify the different individuals based on where they lived through the use of Zip codes," Ms. Sweeney said. "They also were able to plug in various other demographic characteristics and come up with a market."

■ The second thing that helped the industry was the credit card. "All of a sudden, people could make transactions over the telephone. Using a number, you were able to make a purchase," she explained. The whole credit card revolution, coupled with the rising use of computers, had a great deal to do with the segmentation of lists and added to the convenience of shopping by mail.

It seemed like overnight. Not only were retail stores putting out catalogs to draw people in, they also were reaching those who couldn't get into the stores. Direct mail catalog companies were popping up in all areas of the country, small local ones and larger far-reaching ones. Ms. Sweeney said that they really have no idea how many catalog companies are in existence, although they can estimate the number of catalogs in the mail and their dollar worth.

Even though the costs of entering the catalog business seem prohibitive when you consider the cost of renting lists, acquiring merchandise and producing a catalog, the industry is still wide open.

Comparative economics show that in spite of the high start-up costs, mail order catalogs are cheaper than maintaining stores and staffs; and mail order companies usually reap a higher profit margin—about 6% on sales to conventional retailer's 3.5%.

Since everything is escalating in cost, there are a number of things happening in the industry. One of those, Ms. Sweeney explained, "is the catalogs are getting better looking, spending more money on graphics. And the companies are paring down their lists and becoming more selective. They are not mailing to as many people as they were before.

"However," she added, "the number of catalogs entering the mailstream every year is increasing because there are more new catalogs coming out every year."

Where books and magazines were some of the earlier entries into the catalog field, many companies are starting up in other specialized fields, everything from expensive gifts to food; from toys to home furnishings. Almost anything can be purchased by mail.

One of the other factors that has helped the increase in the direct mail catalog business is the rise in the number of working women— who have less time to shop. "There is a significant number of people who have been displaced from the traditional shopping habits," said Ms. Sweeney.

Karl Hopper, of the Peachtree Report mail order catalog said, "There is no time frame on shopping by mail. Someone who can't sleep at night can get up at three o'clock in the morning and do his shopping."

As the industry becomes more sophisticated, the consumers can be identified more specifically. In an area where demographics once reigned supreme, the area of psychographics has become one of extreme importance.

Information from Zip codes can indicate a certain style of life. Other factors that can be fed into computers include what credit cards you hold; what magazines you subscribe to; if you ever bought by mail; how much you purchased and how often, as well as what type of merchandise.

■ The mailing list is one of the most important assets of a catalog company. The lists can be started from scratch by advertising the catalogs or they can be selected and rented from a number of sources including credit card companies, magazine subscription services, existing competing catalog companies and list brokers.

One other main ingredient has helped push the mail order catalog business into the fastest growing segment of the retail industry and that is energy, an increasingly scarce commodity.

"It is obviously affecting the consumers' ability to get around," said Ms. Sweeney. "The response is already being felt in the retail business. The suburban malls were already experiencing slow months in the summer.

But, she indicates that not all of the malls' lost business goes straight to direct marketers. "I don't think you necessarily can say that the people who aren't going to malls are shopping by mail. There is a real definite feeling about the economy that is keeping people from buying.

Roger Horchow, head of the famous Horchow Collection, agreed in part. "My best selling items this year were mostly useful things and things that people could perceive as having intrinsic value, gold jewelry, for example. We neither offered or sold very many things that were frivolous."

■ The growth of the catalog business has been reflected in another way. The membership of DMMA has been growing, with 500 new members added this year. "All you have to do," said Ms. Sweeney, "is look at our membership roster to know that direct marketing is an enormous and powerful marketing tool. Our roster runs from American Express to Horchow to Shell Oil. Even banks, which are the most stoic marketers, are offering things through the mail."

Shopping from catalogs seems to be a thing of the present. Mail order companies are recognizing that consumer responsibility is one of the most important considerations.

Ms. Sweeney said, "No matter what merchandise you carry, or how beautiful your catalog is, the most important thing to do is to make your customer happy. You must fill your orders on time and give prompt, courteous service."

# The King of Catalogs

## BY ELISA KAPLAN

DALLAS—He's been called the King of the Catalogs, Mr. Santa Claus, Dallas' Greatest Bookmaker and the Catalog Miracle Man, and when asked how it feels to be a household word, he says, "It's kind of . . . so what! As long as it helps the book."

The man is S. Roger Horchow and the book is his story—the confessions of a catalog king—which the book may be named. Horchow is the owner of the Horchow Collection, one of the most successful, if not the most successful mail order catalog business today.

The story of how Mr. Horchow came to be the catalog king is full of simple turns and surprises. He started in retailing as a young man, working summers for the Federated department stores, while attending Yale.

After a three-year stint in the army, he was back into retail and merchandising, this time at Federated's Houston store, Foley's. After a couple of years, he was an assistant gift buyer. After spending eight years with Foley's, Mr. Horchow moved to Dallas and went to work for Neiman-Marcus.

The move to Dallas included not only a new store, but a new wife, the former Carolyn Pfeifer, a Bloomingdale's buyer from Little Rock. In the subsequent years, Mr. Horchow climbed the ladder from buyer to group merchandise manager to a vice-president.

In 1968, he left Neiman-Marcus to head the Boston-based Design Research. A year later, Horchow returned to Neiman-Marcus, this time as vp of mail order, working directly under the chairman of the board, Edward Marcus.

Mr. Horchow was surprised he was allowed to return to Neiman-Marcus, but felt that the return held promise. However, things weren't moving quickly enough and in 1971, when it was evident that Mr. Marcus wasn't ready to retire, Mr. Horchow was ready to move on.

It was about this time that he received a call from Robert Kenmore, head of Kenton Inc., which owned such companies as Cartier's, Mark Cross and Georg Jensen. It seemed that Kenton wanted to start a mail order company and Mr. Horchow was asked to do it.

The prestigious catalog was one of the first of its kind offering designer merchandise in one book Mr. Horchow operated the mail order business out of Dallas, not out of New York where the rest of the corporation was based.

Start-up costs for the mail order business, including building a warehouse, purchasing a mailing list, acquiring an inventory, etc., cost the company $1,000,000 per year for the first two years. Those costs, coupled with the fact that Kenton wasn't doing well financially, forced Mr. Kenmore to sell the whole thing, including the Kenton Collection, as the catalog was called, to Meshulum Riklis.

Mr. Riklis started disposing of

**This year's Christmas edition of the Horchow Collection came in two issues. Trifles is a spin off from the successful Horchow Collection.**

the companies, one by one, and Mr. Horchow convinced Mr. Riklis to sell him the Kenton Collection for $1,000,000 plus a percentage. Mr. Horchow borrowed money from everyone he could; family, friends, prep school and college buddies and even his doctor.

Finally, in 1973, Roger Horchow had what he wanted—his own mail order catalog business.

Mr. Horchow involved his wife and three daughters in the catalog and in early 1974, changed the name to the Horchow Collection. The name change brought with it an increase in sales and he soon was able to pay back all that he had borrowed, with interest.This year, Mr. Horchow expects combined sales of the Horchow Collection catalog and the nearly two-year-old addition to the family, "Trifles," to total $35,000,000.

"It's been the best fall season we've had in our history," the 51-year-old catalog exec said. "It's not the best year we've had, but the fall season is by far the best."

The Horchow Collection is mailed 12 times a year, with two of the catalogs timed for the Christmas season. Between 1,000,000 and 1,500,000 catalogs are mailed each month, and 2,000,000 Christmas catalogs are sent. Approximately 20,000 are mailed overseas each month as well.

"We get a lot of orders from overseas. Most of them are from the very wealthy. They have their orders flown in," Mr. Horchow said.

Besides the Horchow Collection, Mr. Horchow has started several other projects, some successful, others not so. Chas. Pfeiffer & Co., a men's clothing catalog that was filled with conservative, Ivy

League type clothing was one of the projects that didn't make it.

■ Trifles, Horchow's second catalog entry into the gift market, is growing faster than the Collection. "It is already up to about $10,000,000. It's already very solid. It is growing faster because we had the Horchow list."

Trifles goes to the same poeople who receive the Collection, except for those who write in and ask specifically for Trifles. This second catalog offers items that, according to Mr. Horchow, "you might see in broader distribution, but you don't have to go to a store to buy."

In Trifles, as with the Collection, Mr. Horchow approves all merchandise that goes into the catalog. "As I've said many times, I wouldn't put anything into those catalogs that I wouldn't buy for someone. I might not buy it for me, but I need to know someone who I would send it to."

Mr. Horchow is presently working on two new projects. The first is working on getting a distributor for his perfume. Called L'Envoi (in French, meaning "the sending"), it sold 1,000 bottles in a month when it was first introduced in the catalog.

The other project is a book club that was started a year ago as an accidental result of a survey of Horchow's customers. "We sent out a questionnaire to find out what our customers had to say about our service because we didn't think we were growing the way we wanted to. We added a throw-away question, said Mr. Horchow, "What else would you like to buy through the mail?" and the answer came back: 'Books.' "

In a second questionnaire, the customers were asked what kinds of books and the book club, featuring "coffee table" type books, was started. The book club now has over 6,000 members and 15,000 are expected by this time next year.

Another one-time successful project was a catalog featuring only American-made products. Mr. Horchow said he received more fan mail on that than any other project.

He has strong feelings about that project. "I found out that where we used to be so snobby as to go to Venice to buy glass, or this or that country had such great bargains, that right in our own backyard, in California or Ohio, they make beautiful things, and now the prices are comparable to the imports. Besides, you don't have to take a trip or speak a foreign language and you can do it by telephone."

■ "It occurred to me," Mr. Horchow continued, "that we need to invest money in this country and there are a lot of craftsmen in this country who need to be encouraged. We may do it again."

For a catalog that does so well, Mr. Horchow said that he really doesn't know that much about his customers. He knows that 70% are women and that 60% of them work.

■ He also knows that they live in exactly the same places that are the centers of population, areas like New York and California. "We

**Roger Horchow's latest venture is the Horchow Book Society which features so-called coffee table books.**

thought that many of our customers lived in apartments, but they don't. Most live in houses."

At one time, Mr. Horchow was considering opening up a chain of outlet stores. He is now operating three, two in Dallas and one in Fort Worth. "We were going to have more, but then we found out that we would have to buy a lot of close-outs and we would have had things in the stores that were never in the catalogs. The three are enough to get rid of everything. I don't even want to go into them. I have been in only one. It gives me a stomach-ache to see what is left. Even though it's just a dozen or six of something."

■ What is next for Roger Horchow? In July, he is expecting the release of his book, which will be called either "Confessions of a Catalog King" or "Elephants in Your Mailbox."

The future of Roger Horchow holds a new, larger warehouse, new projects, a new book.

After that? Maybe elephants in everyone's mailbox, perhaps?

# She Wished to Be Queen

BY ELISA KAPLAN

DALLAS—If Roger Horchow is known as the "King of the Catalogs," Susan Love Edmonson is the woman who could have been queen.

Starting with nothing, she managed to build one of the most successful gift catalogs in existence, only to end up in bankruptcy court.

The story of the demise of Kaleidoscope, Mrs. Edmonson's catalog company, is not finished and many of the questions as to what happened go unanswered still.

According to Paul Lieberman and Jim Stewart, staff writers on the *Atlanta Constitution,* in a story that pretty well describes what happened, the records do not show "the real-life story of the owner; how she and a handful of the kids started up a $21 billion mail order business; how, when the lights went out and the phones were yanked, she was building new dreams and a new mail order company, and how it all turned sour. How the kids who thought they had gotten in on the ground floor were told to lie and use deceit. How the best inventory (not yet paid for in most cases) was suddenly trucked away to the new mail order company, which seemed to inherit everything but the debts."

■ What is fact and what is fiction in this strange story is hard to discern. One person says one thing, another says something else. What it gets down to is a court battle that still is going on and rumors and speculation that the owner may be indicted for bankruptcy fraud in the criminal courts.

While all that carries on, Mrs. Edmonson is in Rio de Janeiro working on a project with the Brazilian government.

Susan Edmonson started on a shoestring in January, 1974. Once a teacher and a psychologist, the Atlanta housewife took a "modest gamble" and started a mail order catalog. She was looking to fill the void in the mail order business, she said. "When I got my first Horchow catalog, I was so excited I almost had a heart attack. Women were just not being approached by anyone other than Horchow and the field was wide open with very little competition."

In a marketing sense, Mrs. Edmonson was right. She caught the wave of rising interest in shopping by mail and she knew who she wanted to reach.

"We started out with a concept that contemporary women had an idea of what their life style was and that it was probably just a little bit above what their life style actually was, in the form of an aspiration to be fashionable in all areas," she said.

She made her debut in July, 1974, with a b&w catalog, 16 glossy pages, that was sent to 30,000 consumers. Sources say that much of the list came from the Horchow Collection, which at first didn't regard her as serious competition, but later on, it has been said, Horchow held some bitter feeling toward her. Nonetheless, she started with a number of handpicked items, reaching out to the women she wanted to entice.

■ Success came slowly. She was operating out of the carriage house behind the home she shared with her husband, Charles Edmonson, an executive with Foote & Davis, a large printing company. Neighbors helped fill orders and the business was on its way.

The following October, she mailed out a more elaborate catalog which reflected her exquisite taste in buying; the response was beyond anyone's dreams. Husband Charles quit his job to work fulltime for the catalog. Friends and neighbors were called in to work for the 24-hour, seven-day operation.

Business picked up and the pace continued, but the atmosphere still was friendly. According to the story in the *Constitution,* one early employe was quoted as saying, "It used to be like a family. We used to have company meetings where we used to hear the success story. You felt you were really going someplace."

In 1974, the company already had accumulated a quarter of a million dollars in sales. This was attributed to Mrs. Edmonson's uncanny ability to buy. "We started out with a balance of merchandise supporting our concept of the fashionable woman. Whether it was great clothes or toys for her kids or the newest in gourmet cookware or the hottest artist to hang on your wall, we offered it. Over the five year period, we jiggled the balance substantially after we learned what worked and at what time of the year," Mrs. Edmonson explained.

While she was handling the creative end of the affairs, her husband was overseeing the business end. With his business experience, he made a competent manager, employes said.

■ The company grew, and some sources say it was because the company grew too fast that it eventually died. It moved to a new warehouse and the success story was being touted everywhere. In 1975, the second year in business, the company reaped $4,000,000 in sales, increased the number of cat-

**After achieving initial success as a general theme catalog, Kaleidoscope began to focus on specific geographical regions such as Thailand and Peru. Staff and photographers flew to the locations as part of each catalog's preparation.**

alogs and was soon recognized as an up and coming enterprise.

Then, two things happened that began the beginning of the end. Mrs. Edmonson started giving each catalog a theme and she and an entourage of photographers, models and aides would be off shooting and buying in many far-away places, and the business itself caused the demise of her marriage.

At first, she and her husband continued to work together, but they argued more and more about the practicality of her ideas. According to the story in the *Atlanta Constitution,* in November, 1977, Charles remarried a Kaleidoscope employe and established his own mail order company, Charles Keath Ltd.

The divorce took weeks to handle—the 50-50 partnership in the company had to be divided. One of the things that happened was that Charles Edmonson gave Susan Edmonson complete ownership of the catalog. What Charles Edmonson received for his half of the shares in Kaleidoscope, according to the *Constitution* article, was "$750,000, secured, in essence, by everything the company owned; all of the stock, its name, trademark, mailing list, all of its inventory equipment, fixtures and accounts receivable. He would get $200,000 down and the balance in quarterly installments."

The extraordinary settlement was coupled with the one thing that has more blame put on it than any other entity: The computer. Before he left Kaleidoscope, Charles Edmonson had decided that what the company needed was a sophisticated computer to keep up with the orders, billings and inventory.

The new system, according to the *Constitution,* cost $245,000 and was programed "at additional costs by a data processing company. Instead of letting the old system run parallel to the new one as a backup, the two systems were simultaneously plugged and unplugged."

Bizarre orders were received and mail order horror stories were the order of the day. The computer went haywire. Customers received duplicate orders, refunds and goodness knows what all else. In a "Dear Customer" letter, according to the *Constitution,* Mrs. Edmonson blamed problems and delays on growing pains. That is when the end was in sight.

■ Jim Stewart, coauthor of the *Atlanta Constitution* article, said that he had spoken with a number of ex-employes, who told him that they were told to tell the customers that everything was on backorder. Even the manufacturers and suppliers were lied to and told that their "check was in the mail."

In 1978, the company chalked up $18,000,000 in sales, but much of that went to pay off Charles Edmonson and much of the rest went for Mrs. Edmonson's buying trips. And in February, 1979, Mrs. Edmonson filed for bankruptcy.

All the while, Mrs. Edmonson told everyone it would be okay. It wasn't.

Apparently, Mrs. Edmonson was already off and away, working on a new mail order venture, also based in Atlanta. The company, known as MOA, was incorporated in December, 1978. The new catalog was to be called the Peachtree Report.

■ Very few people were even aware of the bankruptcy filing. Richard Handlin, vp-client services at Glenn, Bozell & Jacobs, the Dallas-based ad agency that handled Kaleidoscope's pr, said he wasn't aware of it all. "I think we were made aware by Photographers Inc. [the Dallas-based company that did the photography for the catalog], either that, or we heard from our Atlanta office. It certainly wasn't in the form of a postcard from Mrs. Edmonson."

■ According to the *Atlanta Constitution,* Mrs. Edmonson then further "shocked the mail order community by sending a letter to many of her creditors boldly asking for advances of merchandise for the new company." Mrs. Edmonson announced the formation of the new company, MOA Corp., 10 days before Kaleidoscope was declared dead.

The repercussions of what happened with Kaleidoscope will continue indefinitely. Frank Scroggins, court-appointed receiver for Kaleidoscope, said that 7,500 customers and creditors have filed for claims in the bankruptcy proceeding.

■ "We have 23,000 actual letters where they have demanded their money back. The total list of creditors is slightly over 60,000. That includes not only customers, but people she bought from. They didn't keep accurate records of their trade payables either, so we sent out notices to everyone she did business with, whether it showed a zero balance or not. Toward the end they didn't post, which is not unusual in a bankruptcy setting."

Presently, the case is in Chapter X proceedings, having been converted from Chapter XI. Which has the effect, according to Mr. Scroggins, of removing the last vestige of control from Mrs. Edmonson.

"In a Chapter XI, under the bankruptcy code, she and the stockholders are the only people who could ultimately come up with a plan, and considering all the circumstances—that she had really abandoned Kaleidoscope—we didn't think that was appropriate, so it was converted to a Chapter X."

■ The case was converted to Chapter X on Sept. 14, 1979. The reasoning was, "in the event we could find someone who was willing to buy it, that we would be in the position to convey goods and title without the consent and cooperation of Mrs. Edmonson and also, in the event we were able to come up with some plan other than liquidation, that we

would be able to present it without her input," said Mr. Scroggins.

"We are going to try to continue to find someone who would take the business over. If we fail to find someone who will make an offer above what we can get by just selling everything, then we'll do that. But there is no one who has any legitimate interest other than perhaps parties we have sued. In other words, MOA Corp. and the Peachtree Report."

Mr. Scroggins said that they may have to go to liquidation. If so, the court will wait until everything is done—the litigation is over and everything has been liquidated—then the money received from the liquidation will be distributed *pro rata* among the creditors who have filed a claim.

The litigation has been opposed rather vigorously and, according to Mr. Scroggins, he has been countersued for slander and other charges by Mrs. Edmonson and MOA.

Mrs. Edmonson, who disagrees about the number of creditors involved (she claims about 3,000) has also left Peachtree and is now working on a project with the Brazilian Government, helping it develop its national resources into consumer products.

■ Karl Hopper, head of MOA and the Peachtree Report, said that they parted on amicable terms and that she left in September. Mr. Hopper said that Mrs. Edmonson hurt his business and after she left, their business started growing faster. "There are a lot of anti-Susan Edmonson people floating around. She was a wonderful buyer and marketer, but she just didn't have the business sense that it took."

The Federal Trade Commission has completed an investigation of the bankruptcy and the company. The Federal Bureau of Investigation is still working on the case—it is on its second investigator.

As one source put it, "The company expanded too rapidly, without the benefit of professional management. It was one of those cases, which we have all seen, where a company almost begins believing its press clips and becomes a victim of its own success. I don't believe Mrs. Edmonson was aware of the trouble she was getting the company into by making the kinds of commitments she was making and spending the kind of money she was spending.

■ "The record speaks for that—it did grow quickly and it was a fairly large concern at the time of the bankruptcy in terms of sales," the source continued. "I don't think that Mrs. Edmonson willfully ran the company into the ground. I think that forever and a day she is going to be the biggest victim of this."

The story is far from ended. Susan Edmonson is off to new projects and some "specialized consulting on a very limited basis"; Frank Scroggins is still trying to find a buyer; Charles Edmonson is happily running his own successful company; Jim Stewart is still looking for information, as is the FBI; Karl Hopper is hoping to build the Peachtree Report into something special in the catalog business and the apathetic creditors simply go on about their business and wait.

# Retail/Mail Order Marriage

## BY B. G. YOVOVICH

CHICAGO—In light of the successful marriages of in-store and mail order marketing that such diverse operations as Frederick's of Hollywood and New York's Metropolitan Museum of Art have enjoyed, increasing numbers of mail order houses and traditional retailers are flirting with the idea of expanding their marketing efforts and embracing the techniques used by their opposite numbers.

"More and more marketers are trying to make it possible for their customers to shop the way that is most convenient for them," says Robert Kestnbaum, who heads a Chicago-based consulting company specializing in direct mail. "The marketer of the future will blend all channels" with both in-store and direct mail playing important roles.

■ On the retail side, the recent gas shortages and rising gas prices have been inhibiting shoppers from traveling to stores, and the increase in the number of working women has pushed retailers to examine direct mail more closely.

By 1985, for example, it is estimated that more than 50% of the women in the U.S. will be employed outside the home, severely cutting into the amount of time they will have for shopping.

"The increase in the number of small and single person households has also meant a reduction in the time available for convenient shopping," adds Maxwell Sroge, who heads his own Chicago-based consulting company. Mr. Sroge points out that major corporations are beginning to realize that technological developments in videodiscs, cable television, telephone technology, and in-home computers all will help to encourage customers to do their shopping from their homes.

■ According to Mr. Sroge, who compiles a variety of statistics for his quarterly and annual reports on the state of the mail order industry, the mail order business is growing at a rate of almost twice that of conventional retailing.

Even for those retailers who have used direct mail in the past, the recent interest in direct mail has resulted in use of more sophisticated efforts.

"Though retailers have used statement inserts and seasonal catalogs for a long time," says Chuck Ransdell, credit sales promotion manager for Federated department stores, "most of the effort was designed to stimulate store traffic. Though they still have a long way to go, department stores have generally become much more sophisticated in their mail operations."

■ Bloomingdale's, part of the Federated network, is one of the more recent retailers to significantly upgrade its mail order operations.

"We started back in August, 1978," recalls Bloomingdale's direct response marketing director Doreen McCurley, "by building a historical file to see if mail order was viable." In July, 1979, Bloomingdale's began accepting American Express cards, enabling Ms. McCurley to test outside buyer lists.

The results were encouraging.

"We found that the Bloomingdale's name was important and that people from all over the country want to buy from Bloomingdale's," says Ms. McCurley.

The store decided to go ahead with further expansion of its mail order program, and, by the fall of 1980, says Ms. McCurley, "We will be setting up a separate mail order profit center and will handle our own operations from procurement to warehousing to fulfillment."

Mail order requires a different type of expertise from that used in retail operations, says Ms. McCurley.

In mail order operations, "you have to learn to edit your merchandise. In a store, for example, you might have two similar-looking blouses, one priced $38 and the other $42. You would never do this in a catalog," says Ms. McCurley, since the customer would invariably choose the less expensive item and "you would lose the $42 sale and waste the space you spent on it."

Ms. McCurley also recommends that retailers avoid trying to sell hard to fit items via mail order.

Copywriting can also be a problem for retailers according to consultants Sroge and Kestnbaum.

"Many retailers still approach catalogs as another form of advertising," says Mr. Kestnbaum, "and they often use too little copy and do not include vital product information."

"You have to keep in mind that the customer is 1,000 miles away," adds Mr. Sroge. "The creative side of direct mail copywriting has to transpose the one-to-one [in-store] relationship onto paper. The copy should anticipate the customer's questions and concerns. In fact, it should anticipate what would normally occur in a face-to-face encounter."

■ On the other side of the marketing coin, many established mail order companies—including such companies as the Brookstone Co., Edmund Scientific, Eddie Bauer and Franklin Mint—have begun to open retail outlets.

"Though it's constantly growing, there are only so many people who will buy merchandise from a catalog," says Jon Medved, marketing manager for the Brookstone Co. "We all live off the same names" in the mail order business, says Mr. Medved, who is also chairman of the Direct Mail/Marketing Assn.'s catalog council, and who says that at the recent DMMA meetings, "the opening of retail outlets has been one of the hottest topics."

■ The Brookstone Co. itself has participated in this trend and has opened retail outlets in an effort to expand from its mail order base. Brookstone's first store at its Peterborough, N.H., headquarters opened in 1973, and the company has added six other stores—in Boston and a Boston suburb, in Philadelphia and a Philadelphia suburb, in Manchester, N.H., and in Atlanta—since fall, 1976.

When opening retail outlets, mail order companies generally locate them in "areas that reflect the profile of your customers," says Steven Lett, vp of Edmund Scientific, a Camden, N.J.-based mail order company that is planning to open its first outlying retail store in the near future.

■ Edmund's new outlet will be located in an area that fits the company's customer profile and is within 200 miles of the company's headquarters and factory outlet.

"We have to move it far away to cut the umbilical cord," explains Mr. Lett, "so that when problems arise, they will have to be solved by the store, independent of the home base."

The expansion into retail operations has been made easier by postal changes.

"The government did us a big favor when it introduced Zip codes," says F.N. Mellinger, president of Frederick's of Hollywood, because "it helped us identify where our customer strengths are."

- The information garnered from Zip codes has helped Mr. Mellinger expand his business from its beginnings as a mail order operation in 1946 to include 118 boutiques in 30 states.

Though locating a store in a high customer area may be attractive. Brookstone's Mr. Medved cautions that, "When opening a store, a catalog mailer must include in his financial equation the loss of mail order business that will result from the retail operation."

The route from mail order to retail has also been suggested as the natural means for developing a market for new and specialized items.

Specialty mail order companies catering to customers dispersed over a wide area can do quite well "in situations in which in-store re-tailers simply could not survive," says consultant Sroge.

According to Mr. Sroge, who was director of planning at Bell & Howell at one point in his career, "companies often have ideas for products that don't fit into the mass marketing distribution channels. Instead of abandoning the products, they can use mail order."

Clothing for large men and women, gourmet accessories and specialized books are some of the areas in which mail order marketing has helped retail operations.

For example, at the Museum of Metropolitan Art in New York, where 65% of the museum's $18,000,000 in annual sales comes through its mail order operations, mail order manager Paul Jones says, "If we had not had the mass market that the mail order operation had given us, we simply could not have published some of our books" because not enough could be sold in the museum's store to make the titles profitable.

"Retail and mail order can work together side-by-side. Neither hinders the other," concludes Bloomingdale's Ms. McCurley. "It's a good marriage."

# What's on the Horizon?

**BY JEFFREY DeBRAY**

NEW YORK—Cable-television subscribers in Columbus, O., and Reston, Va., are participating in a unique experiment that could dramatically alter the nature of direct marketing.

Warner Amex Cable Communications Inc., a subsidiary of Warner Communications Inc. in which American Express Co. recently purchased a 50% stake, is offering subscribers a video catalog channel that features products from an American Express catalog.

"This represents the first time that a separate cable tv channel has been reserved solely for the purpose of merchandising," said Robert G. McGroarty, vp-marketing, for Warner Amex. These subscribers "now have the option of conducting all their shopping from the comfort of their homes," he says. Well, perhaps, not all their shopping—such products as housewares, jewelry and sportswear are displayed at five-minute intervals throughout the day—but it does represent a departure from traditional direct marketing through newspapers, direct mail and television.

While the number of homes reached through this experiment is limited—by conservative estimates it is well under 100,000 households—the implications for future direct marketing are wide, and it could be during the 1980s that such methods gain wider acceptance.

"Two-way communications will certainly change the face of direct marketing," says Bob Sawyer, senior vp, AyerDirect, N W Ayer in New York. "People have been talking about it for a long time, but it is the technology and equipment that are the key to it and to reaching as many people as possible."

A growing breed of technology such as videodiscs, viewdata, tv text, Warner's Qube (through which the video catalog channel is offered) and the increasingly more common cable are changing the ways in which direct marketers view potential consumers and how they go about enticing them. At the forefront of this potentially explosive field is Qube, which is available only in Columbus, O., and reaches about 30,000 homes. "This is not television. It is not even cable television as we know it," says Gustave M. Hauser, cochairman and chief operating officer of Warner Amex. "It is the next step—a supermarket of electronic services."

Qube allows subscribers to take part in opinion polls, rate performers and a host of other activities through a small home console that is attached to the tv and enables them to interact with a program or ad.

While Warner officials are understandably enthusiastic about their venture, there is strong support among others in the direct response field for the possibilities that this technology will allow.

One of the most outspoken proponents of the use of such technology is Lester Wunderman, chairman of Wunderman, Ricotta &

Kline, a direct response agency based in New York." The '80s will be the direct marketing decade. It will be a whole new way of shopping. People will opt to shop at home instead of in the store. It could change the face of retailing," he says.

Mr. Wunderman says he doesn't think much more technology will be needed than already exists. "It won't take anything more except the profit motive to get going even more," he declares. "The laws of the marketplace will let it happen. No laws or regulation will be needed. The day computerization was developed this was all inevitable."

Less sanguine, although still enthusiastic about the possibilities that technological advances will permit direct marketers, is Donna Sweeney, who handles public relations for the Direct Mail/Marketing Assn."The industry is talking about it but it is still in the developmental stage. It's sort of like when Henry Ford invented the car—it took several decades to catch on."

The direct response industry, which generated some $87 billion in revenues in 1978, the latest year for which figures are available, is closely monitoring the initial moves into the use of two-way systems, but it "probably won't catch on until the end of the '80s, and

then in a limited way," says Ms. Sweeney.

Mr. Sawyer of AyerDirect, whose agency handles such accounts as the U.S. Army, Pan Am, 7UP and American Telephone & Telegraph Corp., agrees. "It probably won't have any great significance until 10 years from now and it is more commercially oriented. It's an evolution that is going to occur over time."

The importance of two-way systems, he says, is that they can "segment and isolate your audience" more than any currently available means, and that "direct marketers will be the first kind of advertisers to enter that market."

Indeed, the increasing cost of direct mail—a popular form of direct response advertising with a 14% share of the market, as opposed to 30% for newspapers and 20% for tv—is almost forcing direct marketers to seek other marketing means.

Laser printing, which has been available for more than two years, has begun to make a significant impact on the direct mail market, but with steadily escalating mailing costs, two-way communications systems are bound to be even more closely scrutinized in terms of cost-efficiency and based on their initial ability to lure consumer dollars.

# What Agencies Think (or) The Agency View

**BY MARY BYRNES**

NEW YORK—Like the Ugly Duckling, it's about to become a swan. That's how direct response agencies view their expanding slice of the industry. And although they may differ about just how high their "swan" can fly—and what will keep it aloft—they do agree that its future is bright.

"It's not junk mail anymore," is the consensus. Better ads, better products and services, and a growing public acceptance of shopping-by-mail-or-phone are key factors.

General trends such as the energy crunch, the popularity of hard-to-find food and hobby items, and working wives with limited time, along with technological advances like the 800 number, have all bolstered the pull of direct response.

"Ten years ago, all we had were records and gadgets," says Ron Bliwas, senior vp at Alvin Eicoff, Chicago, broadcast specialists, whose clients now range from Roll-o-Mop to Avon and Time-Life Books. "And we're convinced you can sell *almost* anything—even big ticket items like cars—by direct response.

"You'll see more and more of this in the future, especially the pairing of direct response with some conventional ad medium. For example, direct response ads on tv or radio may refer the consumer to print ads in local papers for additional information. Or a sales letter may be followed up with a phone call or a personal visit."

Ayer Direct account exec Troy Ellen Dixon also sees direct response "coming into its own at last" with wider use and more products and services to sell. "The major agencies are already taking note of the potential of direct response," she says, pointing to the number of recent acquisitions of small direct response shops by large full-service agencies. In the near future, she predicts, every major agency will have a direct response arm.

"It's very exciting to see direct response—which has been undervalued for so long—finally getting some of the action."

At the Direct Marketing Agency, Stamford, Conn., president Norman Suslock sees a growth in the use of traditional direct mail advertising. Word processing and more

selective mailing lists, he says, will make this tried-and-true medium more potent than ever before.

"There's not much of the old 'junk mail' around anymore," he insists. "Mailing pieces have become slicker, more sophisticated, more in tune with the kind of consumer they're trying to reach. And the public tends to view them not as an intrusion, but as a real shopping service—and as information."

At Ogilvy & Mather Direct Response, president Jerry Picholtz sees a future when traditional direct mail methods will yield to new electronic modes of communication, such as two-way television. Videocassettes will be the catalogs of the '80s. And the changes won't be confined just to media.

■ The growing service industry, including professional services—such as legal, dental and health care—are "natural," says Mr. Picholtz, for direct response.

"Our time has come," says Mr. Picholtz. "Direct response at last is in a position to change the unglamorous stepchild image it's always had. That's already beginning to happen, but I think we have to a help it along.

"Our research tells us that sincerity is the quality most lacking in direct response advertising today. That's what creates the 'junk mail' image. If we want to really grow out of our infancy into adulthood, we've got to produce more high-quality direct response ads, ads that are as good as the best in the mainstream of advertising."

# Order Your Direct Marketing Crain Books Library Now!

Get your share of this exploding $82 billion marketing field! These up-to-the-minute books provide you with the concentrated expertise of the outstanding practitioners of the techniques that will be leading the way in the decade of the '80s. Equally useful for small, medium and large firms, direct marketing can solve marketing problems that seem insoluble! Put it to work with these clearly written manuals for success.

| | | | | |
|---|---|---|---|---|
| _____ | CB 006 | Successful Direct Marketing Methods. Revised 2nd Edition. By Bob Stone | Cloth | $24.95 |
| _____ | CB 033 | Profitable Direct Marketing. By Jim Kobs. | Cloth | $19.95 |
| _____ | NB 815 | Direct Mail: Principles and Practices | Paper | $ 2.95 |
| _____ | CB 852 | Direct Marketing (The best of Section 2 in Ad Age). | Paper | $ 4.95 |

**CRAIN BOOKS**

**Order your copy NOW!**
Mail to: Crain Books/740 Rush St./Chicago, Il 60611
Please send books checked above. Enclosed is my check for _____. (Illinois residents please add 6% sales tax.) Please add $1.25 postage and handling for one book and 75¢ for each additional book.

☐ Please send complete catalog of Crain Books.

My name _____

Firm _____

Address _____

City _____ State _____ Zip _____